Arts: A Third Level Course

The Nineteenth-century Novel and its Legacy   Units 18–19

Jude the Obscure

Prepared by Merryn Williams
for the Course Team

The Open University Press

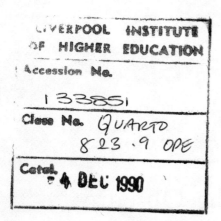
The Open University Press,
Walton Hall, Bletchley, Bucks.

First published 1973.

Designed by the Media Development Group of the Open University.

Printed in Great Britain by
MARTIN CADBURY PRINTING GROUP.

SBN 0 335 00822 4

This text forms part of the correspondence element of an Open University Third Level Course. The complete list of units in the course is given at the end of this text.

For general availability of supporting material referred to in this text, please write to the Director of Marketing, The Open University, Walton Hall, Bletchley, Bucks.

Further information on Open University courses may be obtained from the Admissions Office, The Open University, P.O. Box 48, Bletchley, Bucks.

CONTENTS

FRONTISPIECE: *William Strang*, Thomas Hardy 1893 (*National Portrait Gallery*)

Introduction

Jude the Obscure is, in the opinion of many distinguished critics, an uncharacteristic and unsatisfactory Hardy novel. For this reason they would think that it has no place in a course about the great novels of the nineteenth century, and that it would be fairer to represent Hardy by an earlier, less controversial book like *The Woodlanders* or *Tess of the D'Urbervilles*. But while I hope very much that you will read some of Hardy's other novels, if you haven't done so already, I think there are special reasons for making a study of *Jude*. We may feel that it's a less perfect achievement than they are, but the point is that *Jude* explores certain profound questions—about education, about religion, about the position of women in society—which were of special importance to its own time and ours. More than any other novel which we have been studying, it dramatizes the questions which more and more people were beginning to ask in the last years of the Victorian era. If we compare *Mansfield Park*, written at the beginning of the century, with *Jude the Obscure*, written at the end of it, we at once realize how enormously the novel had changed and how people's ideas about many basic issues had been transformed.

I don't mean by this that *Jude* was in any way an average novel of its time. When it came out in 1895 it caused the greatest literary scandal for many years, was banned from public libraries and was thrown in the fire by a bishop. Hardy tells us something about this in the 1912 Postscript, and I have included a selection of reviews at the back of the Unit so that you can read them for yourself. It's worth thinking about why *Jude* shocked and upset its first readers. Obviously they must have felt that Hardy was undermining their values ('Throughout the book a great many insulting things are said about marriage, religion, and all the obligations and relations of life which most people hold sacred',)[1] but was this really the case?

The problem goes deeper than one of treatment. Hardy caused great offence by the scenes involving Arabella and the pigs, but I think that even if he had left them out the book would still have been attacked for the same reasons. Another thing to which people objected was Hardy's frankness about sex. Unlike the French (though like the Americans and Russians) English novelists had a long tradition of reticence, and Hardy's attempts to describe Jude's and Sue's sexual problems were very bold for his time. Words like 'coarse', 'gross', 'revolting', were freely used by his critics, and if Hardy in 1973 seems extremely restrained (he says in a letter, reprinted in Section 6 (p. 49), that he was only allowed to hint at Sue's frigidity) this should not blind us to the fact that *Jude* was a more outspoken novel than any reputable English work for the previous hundred years.

But, as I said, it wasn't only a question of treatment. Where Hardy deeply shocked his public was in questioning certain assumptions on which their whole code of morals was based. In *Jude* he stated boldly that sexual problems existed and that there were no easy answers to them; that orthodox religion was useless or worse than useless in solving these problems; and, although here he was less definite, that the very framework of society was deeply corrupt. 'I perceive there is something wrong somewhere in our social formulas,' says Jude (and it is hard not to feel that he is echoing Hardy's own thoughts); 'what it is can only be discovered by men and women with greater insight than mine—if, indeed, they ever discover it—at least in our time' (p. 338). It sounds vague to say that there is 'something wrong somewhere', but what is wrong is not

---

[1] From a review in *The Guardian*, reprinted in Laurence Lerner and John Holmstrom (eds.), *Thomas Hardy and his Readers*, Bodley Head, 1968, p. 112.

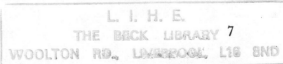

just the fact that the universities were closed to working men at this time. The real trouble, Hardy seems to be suggesting, is that society forces people to behave in ways which are alien to what they want:

'I have been thinking [Sue reflects] . . . that the social moulds civilization fits us into have no more relation to our actual shapes than the conventional shapes of the constellations have to the real star-patterns. I am called Mrs Richard Phillotson, living a calm wedded life with my counterpart of that name. But I am not really Mrs Richard Phillotson, but a woman tossed about, all alone, with aberrant passions, and unaccountable antipathies. . . .'

(p. 214)

Just as Sue finds it impossible to fit into the social mould of Phillotson's wife, so Jude finds it impossible to fit into the recognized pattern as a baker's apprentice, building worker, or husband to Arabella. When the Master of Bibliol writes to him that 'you will have a much better chance of success in life by remaining in your own sphere and sticking to your trade than by adopting any other course' he knows very well that this is 'terribly sensible advice' (p. 125). But, like Sue, he can only be sensible at the cost of outraging his deepest feelings, because they both have 'aberrant passions, and unaccountable antipathies', which get in the way of their doing the expected thing. We can see how important this theme is from two of the titles which Hardy thought of using: *The Recalcitrants* and *Hearts Insurgent*. In the 1912 Postscript he defined the problems of Jude and Sue as 'the forced adaptation of human instincts to rusty and irksome moulds that do not fit them'. Look back at Sue's remarks about 'social moulds', and you will see how similar the language of the two passages is.

Now of course there was nothing new in a novelist writing about people who rebel against social conventions. But in a novel like *Mansfield Park*, for example,

Thomas Hardy, c. 1892
(By courtesy of L. Harrison Matthews)

characters such as Maria Bertram and the Crawfords who question or ignore the sexual and religious assumptions of their society are heavily punished with the author's complete approval. In *Jude*, on the other hand, the author seems to be saying that although the rebels are crushed they are right and society wrong. (We see a different kind of solution to the same problem in *Middlemarch*, where George Eliot shows Dorothea and Lydgate being forced painfully to adapt themselves to a society for which they are not suited—'the mixed result of young and noble impulse struggling amidst the conditions of an imperfect social state, in which great feelings will often take the aspect of error, and great faith the aspect of illusion'.)[1]

This, I think, was the real reason why most of the critics found Hardy's novel outrageous. It wasn't just prudery; it was more a feeling that Hardy was asking too many questions and that the questions went too deep. What exactly these questions were is something we shall have to look at in detail in Sections 2–4. Hardy himself seems not to have thought that he was writing anything particularly revolutionary and to have been taken by surprise at the response to his book. As he said in the Postscript:

In my own eyes the sad feature of the attack was that the greater part of the story—that which presented the shattered ideals of the two chief characters, and had been more especially, and indeed almost exclusively, the part of interest to myself—was practically ignored by the adverse press of the two countries; the while that some twenty or thirty pages of sorry detail deemed necessary to complete the narrative, and show the antitheses in Jude's life,[2] were almost the sole portions read and regarded.

The experience, he claimed, cured him of any further interest in fiction, and *Jude* was his last novel. For the remainder of his life he concentrated on writing poetry, some of it very fine. In his later years he disliked being described as a novelist, and felt that his poetry would last much longer.

In this Course we have deliberately tried not to give potted biographies of novelists which might distract your attention from their novels. But in the case of *Jude* it does help if we know a few facts about Hardy and the society in which he lived. His lifetime (1840–1928) spanned some of the greatest changes in English society—the later stages of the Industrial Revolution, the First World War and the rise of the modern working class. These years saw the completion of the railway system; the founding of the first trade unions; the shift from a mainly rural to a mainly urban culture; the coming of universal suffrage and free education; the decline of religion among the city poor and among intellectuals; and the passing of the new divorce laws in 1857.

Hardy was born and spent most of his life in Dorset, one of the most rural and 'backward' of English counties. But he had lived for five years in London when he was a young man, training to be an architect, and after his novels began to be read he spent three or four months there nearly every year. The people he mixed with ranged from bishops and future Prime Ministers to the atheist and republican poet Swinburne, and Leslie Stephen, author of *An Agnostic's Apology* and father of Virginia Woolf. But he was also in constant touch with people of a very different sort: the working people of Dorchester and the scattered villages round it, and his great novels were written about people like these.

[1] Finale of *Middlemarch*, Penguin edition, 1970.

[2] By this he meant the story of Jude's relationship with Arabella, beginning when she throws the pig's flesh at him and culminating in the pig-killing scene. These two episodes attracted more comment than anything else in the novel.

His experiences in London high society left very little mark on his work. But he was very aware of what the intellectuals in London were thinking, and many of his novels were written with their ideas in mind. It was a paradox. He was living in, and writing about, a remote and old-fashioned community for which he always had a deep affection, yet he was also a keen and sometimes cruel thinker who found himself questioning most of the traditions in which he had been raised. For example, he had been soaked as a child in the ceremonies of the Church of England, but the work of Darwin and Huxley had made it impossible for him to accept the old kind of religion. He had grown up in a village where most people spent their entire lives, before the railway came to Dorchester, but by the time he wrote *Jude* the children of agricultural workers were leaving the villages in tens of thousands to find work in the towns. They never came back, and the old-style village community was destroyed for ever.

I think we must bear these facts in mind when we read about *Jude's* religious struggles, and about the bleakness of life in Marygreen[1] which impels him to try to get away. In this sense he is typical of the countless numbers of young people who were leaving the English villages, during the years when Hardy was writing novels, in search of what they thought was a richer life in the towns. It wasn't common for them to want to go to Oxford, but it *was* common for them to go to night school and read everything they could get hold of (look at the description on pages 314–15 of the Artisans' Mutual Improvement Society in Aldbrickham, whose members are bound together by a 'common wish to enlarge their minds'). Hardy goes out of his way to stress Jude's representative quality:

By caring for books he was not escaping commonplace nor gaining rare ideas, every working man being of that taste now.

(p. 73)

When Hardy began to write *Jude* he was already an established novelist with several fine books to his credit. But the critics were attacking him for becoming increasingly gloomy and satirical (you can see what I mean from parts of Edmund Gosse's review in Section 6). His latest novel, *Tess of the D'Urbervilles, A Pure Woman*, had been criticized quite fiercely because the heroine was a girl who had been seduced and some people felt that it was perverse to describe her as 'pure'. (You can see how this fits in with Hardy's idea, discussed in *Jude*, that the social roles which are forced on human beings bear no relation to what they really are.) After this he began to plan a new book about 'a young man who could not get into Oxford'. The original idea was that he should commit suicide.

When he first modified this plan, and introduced what has been called 'the marriage theme', we don't know. But the writing of *Jude* coincided with a time of intense unhappiness for Hardy. His marriage to Emma Gifford had been strained for years and, although they stayed together until she died, their relationship became worse and worse as she developed a form of religious mania and Hardy became more hostile to the Church. (It's not surprising that Mrs Hardy was very upset by *Jude* and tried to get the publisher to stop it.) Also, in 1890, his cousin Tryphena Sparks died. Hardy had been engaged to her as a young man when she was a student teacher, and although the engage-

---

[1] See Arnold Kettle's comments in his essay on Hardy in the Course Reader, Arnold Kettle (ed.) *The Nineteenth-century Novel: Critical Essays and Documents*, Heinemann Educational/The Open University Press, 1972.

Tryphena Sparks
(Dorset County Museum)

ment was broken off and she married someone else he never forgot her.[1] We know that her memory must have had some influence on *Jude* from Hardy's note in the Preface:

The scheme was jotted down in 1890, from notes made in 1887 and onwards, some of the circumstances being suggested by the death of a woman in the former year.

It has also been suggested[2] that the picture of Sue was inspired by another woman, Florence Henniker, whom Hardy met when he was planning *Jude*. She was an authoress, though not such a brilliant one as Hardy seems to have thought, and he described her as 'a charming *intuitive* woman'. She was married and discouraged him from falling in love with her, but they remained close friends for several years.

It is dangerous to read too much into these facts, although it is certainly a good thing to know them, as a few among many other facts which may have had some influence on *Jude*. But I think you will agree with me that we cannot read the novel without being aware of a sense of deep unhappiness in Hardy's presentation of 'the fret and fever, derision and disaster, that may press in the wake of the strongest passion known to humanity'.

[1] Hardy's relationship with Tryphena, which only came to light recently, is discussed in *Providence and Mr Hardy*, Hutchinson, 1966, by Lois Deacon and Terry Coleman, and in F. R. Southerington's *Hardy's Vision of Man*, Chatto and Windus, 1971. One suggestion is that they had an illegitimate son, who inspired the figure of Little Father Time.

[2] By F. B. Pinion and Evelyn Hardy in *One Rare Fair Woman*, Macmillan, 1972.

1   THE METHOD OF THE NOVEL

Of course the book is all contrasts—or was meant to be in its original conception. Alas, what a miserable accomplishment it is, when I compare it with what I meant to make it!—e.g. Sue and her heathen gods set against Jude's reading the Greek testament; Christminster academical, Christminster in the slums; Jude the saint, Jude the sinner, Sue the Pagan, Sue the saint; marriage, no marriage; etc., etc.'[1]

This is an important statement of Hardy's own attitude to his novel. We can read it together with his description of *Jude* in the Preface as the story 'of a deadly war waged between flesh and spirit' (a statement which we'll be examining more closely in Section 4) as a summing-up of what the novel is all *about*. In this Section I want to look at some examples of Hardy's language and imagery and discuss the question of what he was trying to do with them. Perhaps you have already heard David Lodge's radio talk which examines the same question from a different point of view.

'The schoolmaster was leaving the village, and everybody seemed sorry.' This sentence, the first in the novel, is one that few of us would notice because it is made up of the extremely pure and simple English which seems so much easier to write than it actually is. If you've read any Hardy criticism, you'll probably have heard a great deal about his 'awkwardness', and it's true that he often wrote things which sound artificial. He was self-conscious about his style, and used to study editorials in *The Times* in the hope of improving it, partly perhaps because he had never been to a university and lacked confidence in the worth of his own education. His attempts to write 'well' probably did him more harm than good; even in his best novels he would occasionally produce a horrible sentence like, 'Can forgiveness meet such a grotesque—prestidigitation as this?' (in *Tess of the D'Urbervilles*) or 'I confess I am utterly stultified in my estimate of you' (*Jude*, p. 363).

I don't think this kind of writing is as typical of Hardy as is the sentence I quoted just now. But just because the *language* of this sentence is so clear it doesn't follow that the *meaning* is simple. Consider for a moment how you would react to: 'The schoolmaster was leaving the village, and everybody *was* sorry.' My own feeling is that this not only sounds weak and sentimental, but also gives precisely the opposite meaning to the one which Hardy wanted. The word 'seemed' is a good example of Hardy's irony; why? Read through the first two pages, as far as 'a better chance of carrying it out than I should have elsewhere' and see if you can find any more places where Hardy is being ironic.

Discussion

Hardy remarks that Mr Phillotson bought a piano with the intention of learning music, but never did so. He also shows us the boy Jude's unhappiness at losing his teacher, but adds:

[1] Hardy, in a letter to Edmund Gosse, 20th November, 1895. See Section 6, p. 49–50.

He was not among the regular day scholars, who came unromantically close
to the schoolmaster's life, but one who had attended the night school only
during the present teacher's term of office. The regular scholars, if the truth
must be told, stood at the present moment afar off, like certain historic disciples,
indisposed to any enthusiastic volunteering of aid.   (p. 14)

The point is made so quietly that we don't take much notice of it, but it does
suggest the possibility that the schoolmaster isn't as nice as he seems. Phillotson
only appears briefly at this stage, and we don't get much idea of what he's
like as a person; the important thing about him is that he plants the Christminster dream in Jude's head. But, as we see when we've read the whole book,
there's a truly remarkable amount of concealed irony in this opening scene.
It foreshadows the fact that Phillotson will give up his scheme of getting a degree
at Christminster, just as he earlier gave up his scheme to learn music, and it
also hints at his obstinate unattractiveness—'A very civil, honourable liver;
but . . . there be certain men here and there that no woman of any niceness
can stomach' (p. 199)—which will turn out to be at the heart of his losing
struggle with Jude over Sue. There's a suggestion, too, that Jude has a tendency
to idealize things and people from a romantic distance, and that he may be in
for some shocks when he comes 'unromantically close'.

This irony of Hardy's (some would call it bitterness, or pessimism) runs right
through his work. It's particularly important in a novel like *Jude* which is in a
sense all about lost illusions or, in Hardy's phrase, 'shattered ideals'. There are
fairly obvious examples of this, like the scene where Jude's lofty dreams of the
future are interrupted by Arabella throwing the pig's flesh in his face, but
there are also others which are less obvious. Take the scene in which Jude
bumps into Mr Vilbert, just after he has been dreaming about the 'wonderful
city' of Christminster:

'I mean to go to Christminster some day.'

'Whenever you do, you say that Physician Vilbert is the only proprietor of
those celebrated pills that infallibly cure all disorders of the alimentary system,
as well as asthma and shortness of breath. Two and threepence a box—
specially licensed by the government stamp.'   (p. 32)

I myself think that the irony in this passage is more successful than it is in the
better-known one, for if Hardy had one real fault it was his tendency to labour a
point which was already obvious. He does this regularly in his descriptions of
Arabella, like this one:

Entering the gate he found that three young unfattened pigs had escaped from
their sty by leaping clean over the top, and that she was endeavouring unassisted
to drive them in through the door which she had set open. The lines of her
countenance changed from the rigidity of business to the softness of love when
she saw Jude, and she bent her eyes languishingly upon him.   (p. 57)

There's irony here all right, but it's of an extremely crude and simple kind,
and by no means on the same artistic level as the irony we were discussing
before. Hardy very often weakens his writing by overstating what he wants to
say, though not always so crudely. Look, for example, at the way in which he
tries to convey the utter dreariness of the ploughed field where Jude works:

The fresh harrow-lines seemed to stretch like the channellings in a piece of new corduroy, lending a meanly utilitarian air to the expanse, taking away its gradations, and depriving it of all history beyond that of the few recent months.   (p. 18)

Having made his point about the dead monotony of the field by comparing it to the lines in corduroy, he goes on to philosophize about it—'lending a meanly utilitarian air to the expanse'—and thus, I feel, destroys most of the sharpness and impact of the image. This is the kind of abstract, 'literary' description for which Hardy had a lifelong weakness. On the other hand we get a much better idea of what it *feels* like to be standing in the middle of a ploughed field from the opening of the previous paragraph:

The brown surface of the field went right up towards the sky all round, where it was lost by degrees in the mist that shut out the actual verge. . . .'

But here, again, he isn't content with simply telling us what the mist looked like and feels obliged to say that it 'accentuated the solitude'.

I want you now to look at a fairly typical passage from Hardy and see what you think of its style. It's a description of Jude's feelings, just after he has left his books and gone on an outing with Arabella:

He walked as if he felt himself to be another man from the Jude of yesterday. What were his books to him? What were his intentions, hitherto adhered to so strictly, as to not wasting a single minute of time day by day? 'Wasting!' It depended on your point of view to define that: he was just living for the first time, not wasting life. It was better to love a woman than to be a graduate, or a parson; ay, or a pope!

When he got back to the house his aunt had gone to bed, and a general consciousness of his neglect seemed written on the face of all things confronting him. He went upstairs without a light, and the dim interior of his room accosted him with sad inquiry. There lay his book open, just as he had left it, and the capital letters on the title-page regarded him with fixed reproach in the grey starlight, like the unclosed eyes of a dead man:

Η ΚΑΙΝΗ ΔΙΑΘΗΚΗ[1]

(p. 54)

Read this through several times and note down anything that you find interesting about the language Do you think that it is well or badly written, and why?

Discussion

I don't know what you felt, but my impression was that there is a very great difference between the first paragraph and the second. The first one is written in a slack, undistinguished style which contrasts sharply with the beautiful and impressive English which follows. We see Jude walking home, absorbed in the sensations of the moment, and Hardy shows us the thoughts passing through his head by means of the rhetorical question, 'What were his books to him?' and the defiant assertion, 'he was just living for the first time, not wasting life'. I wonder whether, like me, you got a strong impression of falseness from this passage. Very possibly it is 'better to love a woman than to be a graduate,

[1] The New Testament.

or a parson . . . or a pope', but we don't feel that Jude has really thought about what he is doing, and certainly not that he loves Arabella. So perhaps it isn't fair to blame Hardy for the shallowness of the writing in this passage; perhaps it is only reflecting the shallowness of Jude's thoughts.

After this, the second paragraph comes as rather a shock. From being inside Jude's mind we suddenly move back to seeing him from the outside, as he gets back to the darkened house 'without a light' and finds the open Bible on the table. He feels that the house is silently accusing him of neglect, and that the book is reproaching him 'like the unclosed eyes of a dead man'. I don't think this means only that the book is written in a dead language; there's also the powerful feeling that, behind all the romping and flirting with Arabella, and however he may choose to ignore it, Death is there, waiting for Jude.

I find it particularly significant that Hardy uses the image of 'the grey starlight' in this passage to remind Jude of what he is doing. We hear about the starlight twice more in the first book, once when Jude tries to drown himself in the icy pond, and once when he goes out again on the Christminster road and his old ambition comes back. There is a feeling throughout that the stars represent something colder, higher, brighter than Arabella and the world of 'the flesh' which is the only thing she understands.[1] (It's worth noting that Hardy takes the motto, 'Save his own soul he hath no star', for the second book, about Jude's adventures in Christminster, and that Sue is described in the same terms. She is 'a kindly star' (p. 97), and 'a woman whose intellect was to mine like a star to a benzoline lamp' (p. 414).)

The stars form part of a whole web of images concerning light and darkness. Look at the description of Jude's first impression of Christminster:

Some way within the limits of the stretch of landscape, points of light like the topaz gleamed. The air increased in transparency with the lapse of minutes, till the topaz points showed themselves to be the vanes, windows, wet roof slates and other shining spots upon the spires, domes, freestone-work, and varied outlines that were faintly revealed. It was Christminster, unquestionably; either directly seen, or miraged in the peculiar atmosphere.

The spectator gazed on and on till the windows and vanes lost their shine, going out almost suddenly like extinguished candles. The vague city became veiled in mist. Turning to the west, he saw that the sun had disappeared. The foreground of the scene had grown funereally dark, and near objects put on the hues and shapes of chimaeras.   (p. 26)

A chimaera is a 'goat with lion's head and serpent's tail; a bogy; a wild impossible scheme or unreal conception' according to the *Oxford English Dictionary*. Christminster is described in terms of light, spires, domes, jewels (like the new Jerusalem in the Book of Revelation whose foundations were made of topaz and other precious stones). But it can only be seen occasionally and through the mist, and Jude may not be seeing the actual city at all, but a mirage. It is beautiful, but is it *real*, in the sense that Jude imagines it? The actual place is real enough, but perhaps Jude's idea of it has no more substance than a dream-city seen in the sky. It doesn't occur to Jude himself to ask these questions at this stage, but I think the reader has to ask them. That is, if he has properly understood the method of Hardy's novel, which is to work through a series of images which illuminate his meaning more fully than direct statements would have done.

---

[1] You might like to think about the way Dickens uses the image of stars in *Great Expectations*.

To make sure that you have grasped what Hardy's imagery is all about, here is an exercise. Make a list of all the images you can remember which Hardy uses to convey an impression of the two women, Arabella and Sue. There's no need to search right through the novel, just read the account of Jude's first meeting with Arabella (pages 43–6) and the early Christminster chapters, where he is becoming aware of Sue without her knowledge. What is Hardy trying to do with these images, and what is the principal contrast between Sue and Arabella?

Discussion

Arabella is always associated with pigs (as David Lodge points out in his radio talk). Hardy also points out that she's a well-developed, 'fleshy' girl—'a complete and substantial female animal—no more, no less' (p. 44). Sue, on the other hand, is first seen in a photograph, wearing 'a broad hat with radiating folds under the brim like the rays of a halo' (p. 84). Jude comes upon her in a religious shop, surrounded by pictures of saints and angels, and afterwards sees her in the cathedral, 'ensphered' by 'harmonies' (p. 99). His first impression of her is of a being associated with light, music, religion; and this is like 'the dew of Hermon' to his soul. Unlike Arabella, she is 'light and slight, of the type dubbed elegant', and her eyes 'combine keenness with tenderness, and mystery with both' (p. 96).

Obviously there's a very great difference in Jude's feeling for the two women, and I think that what Hardy is trying to convey through these images is that, while Arabella appeals only to Jude's animal nature, Sue represents everything that he yearns for on a spiritual and emotional plane. At first he hardly thinks of her sexually at all—she is a 'half-visionary form' (p. 97).

But these descriptions of Sue, like the rest of Hardy's novel, are shot through with irony, and we certainly aren't meant to regard her in the same uncritical way as Jude does. 'A sweet, saintly, Christian business, hers!' he thinks (p. 95), when he sees her designing the church text. But if Hardy had really thought that Sue was sweet and saintly, he was not the kind of writer to express it in such an obvious way. And there's a strong suggestion, in these scenes, that Jude is idealizing her just as he idealized Christminster, without really knowing much about her. When we see her directly for the first time (pp. 99–103) we get a rather different impression. Read this and see what it tells you about Sue.

Discussion

Sue, whom Jude fondly imagines to be the perfect Christian, smuggles some naked statues of the pagan Gods into her room pretending that they are saints. ' "Well, anything is better than those everlasting church fal-lals!" she said' (p. 101). It throws an interesting light on her character that, although she works in a religious shop and goes to church, she is a secret unbeliever. Like the first scene we looked at, between the boy Jude and Phillotson, this is a more ironic and revealing episode than it might at first seem. We've seen already that if Jude has one dominant quality it's the headstrong way that he rushes into emotional commitments—to his studies, to Christminster, to Arabella, to Sue. But the impression we get from this scene is of a girl who is nervous of committing herself to anything, and in this respect is the opposite of her cousin. 'They seemed so very large now that they were in her possession, and so very naked. Being of a nervous temperament she trembled at her enterprise . . . and seemed almost to wish that she had not bought the figures' (p. 101).

Having bought them, she doesn't have the courage of her convictions and is obviously frightened of letting Miss Fontover know what they are.

I hope that studying these passages will have given you some insight into what I have called Hardy's irony—the way in which he incorporates several layers of meaning within a single, and apparently simple, scene. This irony culminates in the marvellous last chapter, when Jude dies in the middle of the Christminster celebrations while Arabella is thinking of 'having a spin there with a fellow's arm round my waist':

The hurrahs were repeated, drowning the faint organ notes. Jude's face changed more: he whispered slowly, his parched lips scarcely moving:

'*Let the day perish wherein I was born, and the night in which it was said, There is a man child conceived.*'

('Hurrah!')

'*Let that day be darkness; let not God regard it from above, neither let the light shine upon it. Lo, let that night be solitary, let no joyful voice come therein.*'

('Hurrah!')

(p. 418)

This is the kind of tension which gives life to the whole novel. Marygreen is real enough; it's a place where pigs are kept and killed and children get beaten for day-dreaming when they should be working, but is Christminster real? Arabella is real flesh and blood, as she makes it clear when she throws her missile in Jude's face, but Sue is 'a sort of fay or sprite—not a woman' (p. 365). Like Christminster, she represents a sort of guiding light to Jude, but they are insubstantial lights which cannot be reached, and which lead him to destruction.

2 CHRISTMINSTER

Lord Rosebery took occasion in a conversation to inquire 'why Hardy had called Oxford Christminster'. Hardy assured him that he had not done anything of the sort, Christminster being a city of learning that was certainly suggested by Oxford, but in its entirety existed nowhere else in the world but between the covers of the novel under discussion. The answer was not so flippant as it seemed, for Hardy's idea had been, as he often explained, to use the difficulty of a poor man's acquiring learning at that date merely as the 'tragic mischief' (among others) of a dramatic story, for which purpose an old-fashioned university at the very door of the poor man was the most striking method; and though the architecture and scenery of Oxford were the best in England adapted for this, he did not slavishly copy them; indeed in some details he departed considerably from whatever of the city he took as a general model.[1]

This should be enough in itself to warn us that Hardy's attitude to Oxford is far from simple. (He had a habit of describing real places under fictional names, and you might like to compare the map of 'Wessex' which appears in *Jude* with the real map of Dorset and the neighbouring counties to see how the two relate.) Yet, as he said, Christminster 'was certainly suggested by Oxford', and the other places in the novel were also suggested by real villages and towns.

[1] F. E. Hardy, *The Later Years of Thomas Hardy*, Macmillan, 1930. Hardy dictated most of this to his second wife, Florence, to be published under her name after his death.

The High, Oxford, looking west (Henry Mimms Collection, Bodleian Library, Oxford)

Fisher Row, Oxford, looking south, about 1900 (Taunt Collection, Oxford City Libraries)

Frank Restall's Coalyard on the Oxford Canal at the end of the nineteenth century (Taunt Collection, Oxford City Libraries)

Magdalene Bridge, Oxford, before widening, 1890 (Henry Mimms Collection, Bodleian Library, Oxford)

Marygreen represents Great Fawley, in Berkshire; Melchester, Salisbury; Shaston, Shaftesbury; and Aldbrickham, Reading.

In spite of Hardy's disclaimer, it does help to know something about the real Oxford and its history if we are fully to understand *Jude*. (You should get some idea of what it looked like in the 1890s from the television programme, and the illustrations in this Unit.) It was, and still is, a very beautiful city, and one can well understand why it reminded Jude of 'the heavenly Jerusalem'. But there were also slummy districts which the tourists rarely saw, such as Jericho (which Hardy calls Beersheba) in the west of the city, the district of the gasworks and the canal and the railway, where most of the working class lived.

Oxford and Cambridge were then, of course, *the* two great English universities (most of what we now call the provincial or redbrick universities hadn't been built). Young men who had been to public school went on to take their degrees there as a matter of course; for a boy with a background like Jude's this was almost impossible. The only subjects studied were theology, mathematics and the classics. There were about twenty colleges where the fellows lived semi-monastic lives (they were all clergymen and were not allowed to marry until the 1870s), but in compensation they led a very comfortable and privileged existence in these ancient buildings.

What was Hardy's attitude to Oxford life? This is a question which we'll have to explore in detail before we can answer it, but I think it is obvious from the first that Hardy's attitude is deeply coloured by the feeling of being an outsider. Most literature about Oxford had been written by men who had been students there; Hardy hadn't, although he had worked in the city helping to design the chapel of the Radcliffe Infirmary. And although both he and the reader are very aware of the Christminster colleges dominating the background of the story, we never get much idea of what life is like in these colleges, because the whole novel is written from the outside looking in.

For a different view of Oxford, from someone who feels *at home* in the university, it's worth looking at the words of Matthew Arnold which Hardy quotes on page 88:

'Beautiful city! so venerable, so lovely, so unravaged by the fierce intellectual life of our century, so serene! . . . Her ineffable charm keeps ever calling us to the true goal of all of us, to the ideal, to perfection'.

It may seem a little strange that a great university should be unaware of 'the fierce intellectual life of our century' (I want to discuss this point in the next Section) but the real pull of Christminster over Jude is not intellectual so much as deeply emotional. Like Arnold he sees it as a gateway 'to the ideal, to perfection', and this makes him reluctant to admit that there could be anything wrong with it:

When he passed objects out of harmony with its general expression he allowed his eyes to slip over them as if he did not see them.   (p. 85)

During his first walk through the city by lamplight he imagines he sees the ghosts of the great men who have been students there. Among them are 'the poet, the last of the optimists', Shelley; 'the smoothly shaven historian so ironically civil to Christianity', Edmund Gibbon; 'the great itinerant preacher' John Wesley; 'the Corn Law convert' Sir Robert Peel; 'the genial Spectator' Addison, and the Tractarian leaders Newman, Pusey and Keble (pp. 86–9). They are so real to him that he finds himself 'speaking out loud, holding conversations with them', until the policeman accosts him and he finds he is almost alone in the city 'so far as solid flesh went'. If we remember that Hardy said the whole novel was about the struggle 'between flesh and spirit', we'll find that this metaphor is significant. Jude characteristically feels that these shadows are more real than ordinary human beings, and it's significant, too (remembering the importance of light/darkness images) that he first sees Christminster in the romantic lamplight, instead of the cruel light of day.

Now turn to page 90 and read the first four paragraphs, as far as '. . . years, weather and man'. What does their language suggest to you about Jude's possible future in Christminster?

Discussion

I think there are two points which emerge from this passage. First, Christminster falls short of what Jude had imagined. 'What at night had been perfect and ideal was by day the more or less defective real.' Looking at it in the daylight for the first time, he sees that several of the buildings are rotting and have a sinister look. There is a strong suggestion that when he knows Christminster better, he will be bitterly disappointed.

Secondly, Hardy stresses that Jude belongs to the class by which the Christminster colleges were built (he starts thinking of 'dead handicraftsmen' now, instead of dead poets and scholars). He finds that the first thing he has to do is get a job, and the suggestion is that his future is not as a student, but as a builder.

Now read on to page 93, as far as 'might some day look down on the world through their panes'. There are three important points which Hardy makes here about Christminster. What are they?

My Answers

(i)   The kind of work done in the stone yard is just as worth while and as noble as that done in the colleges.

(ii)   Not only that, but the world represented by the colleges is dead. The modern world is hostile to everything Christminster stands for.

(iii)   The university is quite unaware that people like Jude exist.

Up to this point we haven't been told very much about Christminster, apart from the obvious fact that it is an ancient and lovely university city (though we did hear that 'there's wenches in the streets o' nights' on page 29). But gradually we are made to realize that in fact there is a quite different Christminster, made up of the people who live in Beersheba and hang round in seedy pubs there—'shop youths and girls, soldiers, apprentices, boys of eleven smoking cigarettes, and light women of the more respectable and amateur class. He had tapped the real Christminster life.' (p. 126). Here is the contrast which Hardy spoke of between 'Christminster academical' and 'Christminster in the slums'.

Jude is finally forced to accept the reality of this contrast when he looks down from the theatre over the city:

One of the O'Shea brothers carving (Oxford University Museum)

From the looming roof of the great library, into which he hardly ever had time to enter, his gaze travelled on to the varied spires, halls, gables, streets, chapels, gardens, quadrangles, which composed the *ensemble* of this unrivalled panorama. He saw that his destiny lay not with these, but among the manual toilers in the shabby purlieu which he himself occupied, unrecognised as part of the city at all by its visitors and panegyrists, yet without whose denizens the hard readers could not read nor the high thinkers live.   (p. 124)

After you've read this passage, I'd like you to have a look at a poem of Hardy's, *The Old Workman*, which was published in 1922 in *Late Lyrics and Earlier* and which you can find in Hardy's *Collected Poems*.[1] Here it is:

'Why are you so bent down before your time,
Old mason? Many have not left their prime
So far behind at your age, and can still
Stand full upright at will.'

He pointed to the mansion-front hard by,
And to the stones of the quoin against the sky;
'Those upper blocks', he said, 'that there you see,
It was that ruined me.'

[1] Thomas Hardy, *Collected Poems*, Macmillan, 1962.

There stood in the air up to the parapet
Crowning the corner height, the stones as set
By him—ashlar whereon the gales might drum
For centuries to come.

'I carried them up', he said, 'by a ladder there;
The last was as big as load a load as I could bear
But on I heaved; and something in my back
Moved, as 'twere with a crack.

'So I got crooked. I never lost that sprain;
And those who live there, walled from wind and rain
By freestone that I lifted, do not know
That my life's ache came so.'

'They don't know me, or even know my name,
But good I think it, somehow, all the same
To have kept 'em safe from harm, and right and tight,
Though it has broke me quite.'

'Yes, that I fixed it firm up there I am proud,
Facing the hail and snow and sun and cloud,
And to stand storms for ages, beating round
When I lie underground.'

Read both pieces through carefully. Can you find a common idea in them both?

Discussion

The similarity goes further than the obvious fact that Jude and the 'old workman' are both stonemasons. The workman has lamed himself for life building a house for people 'who don't know me, or even know my name'. In the same way, it is people like Jude who built Christminster in the Middle Ages and who now keep the colleges in repair. They are 'unrecognised as part of the city at all', but if it were not for their labour 'the hard readers could not read nor the high thinkers live'. In fact, there is another point of contact between the novel and the poem which you couldn't have seen from the short extract I quoted. Jude also strains himself too hard in his work as a builder, and this leads to his final fatal illness:

'Moving the blocks always used to strain me, and standing the trying draughts in buildings before the windows are in, always gave me colds, and I think that began the mischief inside'.   (p. 413)

So Hardy definitely seems to be making the point that, although Christminster ignores and exploits these people, it couldn't exist without them. 'What was most required by citizens? Food, clothing and shelter' (p. 40)—and the stonemasons are seen as providing the 'shelter' which is necessary to life.

Now read this passage:

He only heard in part the policeman's further remarks, having fallen into thought on what struggling people like himself had stood at that Crossway, whom nobody ever thought of now. It had more history than the oldest college in the city. It was literally teeming, stratified, with the shades of human groups,

Interior of the building of
Oxford University Museum
(Oxford University Museum)

who had met there for tragedy, comedy, farce; real enactments of the intensest kind. At Fourways men had stood and talked of Napoleon, the loss of America, the execution of King Charles, the burning of the Martyrs, the Crusades, the Norman Conquest, possibly of the arrival of Caesar. Here the two sexes had met for loving, hating, coupling, parting; had waited, had suffered, for each other; had triumphed over each other; cursed each other in jealousy, blessed each other in forgiveness.

He began to see that the town life was a book of humanity infinitely more palpitating, varied and compendious than the gown life. These struggling men and women before him were the reality of Christminster, though they knew little of Christ or Minster. That was one of the humours of things. The floating population of students and teachers, who did know both in a way, were not Christminster in a local sense at all.   (p. 126)

Does this remind you of a description of a place in Marygreen, earlier in the novel? If you can't remember, turn back to page 18 in the novel (last paragraph) and make notes on any ways in which the two passages seem to be saying the same thing.

Discussion

Hardy is saying that the cornfield at Marygreen, like the city crossroads, has been the scene of intense relationships between people, although this is not obvious. He seems to be suggesting in both places that the history of ordinary people, though it isn't written down like the history of Christminster colleges, is every bit as real, valuable and interesting—if not more so. In fact this was a belief which Hardy held very strongly throughout his life. Perhaps you have already read his well-known poem, *In Time of the Breaking of Nations*, written during the First World War. In it he describes a man and a horse ploughing; a bonfire in the countryside; a girl walking with her lover—and concludes that these, not the war, are the most important things in life.

So Hardy put a high value on the ordinary people of Christminster, even though they are 'obscure', like Jude, and very often drunk and disreputable. 'It is an ignorant place', Sue says, in one of her many arguments with Jude, 'except as to the townspeople, artisans, drunkards and paupers. . . . *They* see life as it is, of course, but few of the people in the colleges do' (p. 158). Jude, on the other hand, continues to 'love the place—although I know how it hates all men like me—the so-called Self-taught' (p. 331). Even after he has given up hope of ever becoming a student he goes on making 'Christminster cakes' and models of Christminster colleges, and dreams of sending his little son to the University. It's not easy to say to what extent Hardy sympathized with his dreams. When Sue, in Book Six, is stranded with the children in a gloomy lodging in Christminster, he obviously has a good deal of sympathy with her feelings:

She thought of the strange operation of a simple-minded man's ruling passion, that it should have led Jude, who loved her and the children so tenderly, to place them here in this depressing purlieu, because he was still haunted by his dream.

(p. 343)

Indeed, in this final section of the novel, *At Christminster Again*, the city begins to seem more and more sinister. We see a procession of doctors—'solemn stately figures in blood-red robes' (p. 335), who as they walk through the thunder remind Little Father Time of the Day of Judgment; a horse being kicked in the stomach; and the people standing shivering in the rain and being pushed about by the police. The little boy is depressed by the place and asks, 'Are the great old houses gaols?' (p. 341). The grim-looking busts of the Roman Emperors, around the theatre, look down at 'the bedraggled Jude, Sue, and their children, as at ludicrous persons who had no business there' (p. 339) and the only shelter they can find is in a dreary alley, known as Mildew Lane, which is overshadowed by the college buildings:

. . . the outer walls of Sarcophagus College[1]—silent, black and windowless—threw their four centuries of gloom, bigotry and decay into the little room she occupied, shutting out the moonlight by night and the sun by day.

(p. 343)

---

[1] 'Sarcophagus', of course, means a tomb.

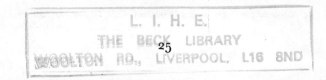

25

Speedwell street, Oxford (Henry Mimms Collection, Bodleian Library, Oxford)

Encaenia procession passing Brasenose College, Oxford, 22 June 1904 (Taunt Collection, Oxford City Libraries)

I want to discuss this part of the novel more fully in Section 5, which is about Hardy's pessimism. But enough has been said to make it obvious that he was very critical of the Christminster colleges, not only because they exclude so many people, but also because they are in some ways intrinsically bad. Are we to think, then, that Hardy had *no* sympathy with Jude's struggles to get into the University, and did he dismiss and despise him as an impractical dreamer? I believe his attitude was a good deal more complicated than this. Hardy could see clearly enough that Jude's dreams were hopeless, and that he hadn't planned his life sensibly, but the fact remains that Jude is the hero of the novel and that Hardy identified with him and his aspirations in a very deep way:

'I don't admit that my failure proved my view to be a wrong one, or that my success would have made it a right one; though that's how we appraise such attempts nowadays—I mean, not by their essential soundness, but by their accidental outcomes . . .'

'. . . Don't tell them that!' whispered Sue with tears, at perceiving Jude's state of mind. '. . . You struggled nobly to acquire knowledge, and only the meanest souls in the world would blame you!'

(pp. 336–7)

I want you now to consider Jude's conversation with the man in Marygreen:

'You've j'ined a College by this time, I suppose?'
'Ah, no!' said Jude. 'I am almost as far off that as ever.'
'How so?'
Jude slapped his pocket.
'Just what we thought! Such places be not for such as you—only for them with plenty o' money'.
'There you are wrong,' said Jude, with some bitterness. 'They are for such ones!'

(p. 121)

In what sense can it be said that Christminster is 'for' obscure people like Jude? If you find this question difficult, look back at his conversation with Sue (pp. 157–8).

Sue, although she likes to mock Jude's ambitions, says:

'You are one of the very men Christminster was intended for when the colleges were founded; a man with a passion for learning, but no money, or opportunities, or friends. But you were elbowed off the pavement by the millionaires' sons.'

(p. 158)

As Hardy sees it, the tragedy of Christminster is that it has lost sight of its real purpose, which is to be open to everyone who can benefit from the education it can give. He is very hostile to the university in its present form; it is a bitter irony that when Jude is dying 'the doctors in the Theatre' should be busy 'conferring honorary degrees on the Duke of Hamptonshire and a lot more illustrious gents of that sort' (p. 422). But I think that, like Jude, he had felt the deep emotional attraction of Oxford (or Christminster) and believed that it was capable of becoming something much better than it was in his day. That's why he made Jude say hopefully:

'I hear that soon there is going to be a better chance for such helpless students as I was. There are schemes afoot for making the University less exclusive, and extending its influence.'   (p. 413)

He also records, in the Postscript, that when Ruskin College was founded for working men some people thought it should have been called the College of Jude the Obscure (and what a pity it wasn't!). I think his final judgement is that Christminster belongs to the ordinary people who live and work there— 'artisans, drunkards and paupers'—whether they want it or not. And Jude, whether or not the University wants him, belongs to Christminster just as much as its more famous sons. Look again at the description of his first walk through the city by lamplight, and then at his conversation with Arabella:

They went along by the silent colleges, and Jude kept stopping,

'What are you looking at?'

'Stupid fancies. I see, in a way, those spirits of the dead again, on this my last walk, that I saw when I first walked here.'

'What a curious chap you are!'

'I seem to see them, and almost hear them rustling. But I don't revere all of them as I did then. I don't believe in half of them. The theologians, the apologists, and their kin the metaphysicians, the high-handed statesmen, and others, no longer interest me. All that has been spoiled for me by the grind of stern reality!'

New College, Oxford, 1913 (Henry Mimms Collection, Bodleian Library, Oxford)

The expression of Jude's corpse-like face in the watery lamplight was indeed as if he saw people where there was nobody. At moments he stood still by an archway, like one watching a figure walk out; then he would look at a window like one discerning a familiar face behind it. He seemed to hear voices, whose words he repeated as if to gather their meaning.

'They seem laughing at me!'

'Who?'

'O—I was talking to myself! The phantoms all about here, in the college archways and windows. They used to look friendly in the old days, particularly Addison, and Gibbon, and Johnson, and Dr Browne, and Bishop Ken——'

'Come along do! Phantoms! There's neither living nor dead hereabouts except a damn policeman! I never saw the streets emptier.'

'Fancy! The Poet of Liberty used to walk here, and the great Dissector of Melancholy there!'

'I don't want to hear about 'em! They bore me.'

'Walter Raleigh is beckoning to me from that lane—Wycliffe—Harvey— Hooker—Arnold—and a whole crowd of Tractarian Shades——'

'I *don't want* to know their names, I tell you! What do I care about folk dead and gone? Upon my soul you are more sober when you've been drinking than when you have not!'

'I must rest a moment', he said, and as he paused, holding to the railings, he measured with his eye the height of a college front. 'This is old Rubric. And that Sarcophagus; and up that lane Crozier and Tudor; and all down there is Cardinal with its long front, and its windows with lifted eyebrows, representing the polite surprise of the University at the efforts of such as I.'

'Come along, and I'll treat you!'

'Very well. It will help me home, for I feel the chilly fog from the meadows of Cardinal as if death-claws were grabbing me through and through. As Antigone said, I am neither a dweller among men nor ghosts. But, Arabella, when I am dead, you'll see my spirit flitting up and down here among these!'

(pp. 406–7)

3   RELIGION

Hardy (you may remember) calls Christminster 'the most Christian city in the country' (p. 101) and in order fully to understand what this means we must again look at the history of nineteenth-century Oxford. The university had always been strongly identified with the Established Church; until comparatively recent times non-members of the Church of England had been kept out, students had to go to chapel every day and all fellows of colleges were in holy orders. But by the 1830s religious life in Oxford and in the Church as a whole had become very shallow, and this gave rise to what was called the Oxford Movement. A group of young dons (variously known as Tractarians, Puseyites, or Anglo-Catholics) began to organize themselves to reform the Church from within, and to make it a more powerful force in the country. The leaders of this movement were John Henry Newman (who described it in his famous book *Apologia Pro Vita Sua*), John Keble and Edward Bouverie Pusey. They were mostly fundamentalists and authoritarians, rather reactionary in politics and very hostile to anyone who wanted to make the Church more liberal. Their attacks on Protestantism (which they associated with the idea of freedom of conscience which could by-pass the central role of the Church) and their liking for ritual in church services caused them to be suspected of too much sympathy for Roman Catholicism. In fact Newman and several of his followers did become Catholics eventually, and after this the movement, as a movement, collapsed.

But its influence went on being felt in Oxford, and indeed in the whole English Church, for many years after that. The religious atmosphere of Oxford was very 'Tractarian' or 'High' at the time Hardy knew it. It is expressed in such places as 'the Church of Ceremonies—St Silas' (p. 353), with its giant crucifix and its odour of incense, where Sue goes after she has begun to break down. This was suggested by St Barnabas' Church, in Jericho, and the giant crucifix can still be seen there today. Miss Fontover's shop has the same sort of atmosphere—'little plaster angels on brackets, Gothic-framed pictures of saints, ebony crosses that were almost crucifixes, prayer-books that were almost missals' (p. 95). As soon as Jude arrives in Chrīstminster he starts to think about the Oxford Movement—some of the phantoms he sees in the streets are 'the founders of the religious school called Tractarian . . . the echoes of whose teachings had influenced him even in his obscure home' (p. 86–7). In the beginning he admires them deeply, as we can see from this conversation with Sue:

'Why must you leave Christminster?' he said regretfully, 'How can you do otherwise than cling to a city in whose history such men as Newman, Pusey, Ward, Keble, loom so large!'

'Yes—they do. Though how large do they loom in the history of the world? . . . What a funny reason for caring to stay! I should never have thought of it!' She laughed. (p. 110)

This neatly pinpoints the intellectual differences between Sue and Jude; it also tells us something about Hardy's own attitude to the religion of Christminster. What is this?

Discussion

We needn't assume that, just because Sue finds Jude's admiration for Newman and Pusey rather funny and old-fashioned, Hardy necessarily agrees with her. After all, most people in the story laugh at Jude, yet most of the time Hardy remains on his side. But I think that he is raising a valid point when he makes Sue ask innocently, 'How large do they loom in the history of the world?' Although she drops it at once, it's a question which calls for a serious answer and it suggests to us that the world is wider than Christminster, and that there are a great many things which the Tractarian movement has left out.

Hardy was attacked many times, both before and after he wrote *Jude*, for abusing religion. I want in this Section to discuss what his religious attitudes really were, and the reason I began by filling in the background to the Oxford Movement was that this is the only *kind* of organized Christianity which he has chosen, in this novel, to discuss.

The Movement was probably the last great religious revival in England. After its impetus had been exhausted most of the best minds turned the other way, and the general drift towards agnosticism was helped by the discoveries of the geologists, and of Darwin, which proved that the Book of Genesis wasn't literally true. Hardy, as we've said, had been brought up in a church-going family, and as a young man he had thought (like Jude) of becoming a clergy-man. But as he grew older he became more sceptical and more critical of religion. It must have seemed to him that the University of Oxford, where so many of the old traditions still lingered, was deliberately blinding itself to facts. Matthew Arnold, you remember, spoke of Oxford as 'so unravaged by the fierce intellectual life of our century', but Arnold, although he too was an agnostic, had admired Newman and wished he could get back his lost faith. Hardy couldn't describe the religion of Oxford in the same nostalgic way. He may well have felt its mysterious charm, but he thought that 'the deadly animosity of contemporary logic and vision' (p. 91) was bound to defeat Tractarianism and everything it stood for.

However, it wasn't only *contemporary* thinking that could be contrasted with Christianity. Hardy was also very sensitive to the tension between the orthodox, Anglican religion of Christminster and the old Greek and Roman religions which are studied within its walls. Sue looks back longingly at these civilizations:

'I feel that we have returned to Greek joyousness, and have blinded ourselves to sickness and sorrow, and have forgotten what twenty-five centuries have taught the race since their time'   (p. 307)

There are two important scenes in the novel in which the characters show affection for the Greek gods. Can you remember what they are?

My Answers

(i)   The first scene is when the sixteen-year-old Jude gets down from his cart and emotionally recites a Latin prayer to the gods of the sun and the moon. He does this under the influence of a beautiful night and the poetry which he has just been reading. Afterwards he is a little ashamed of himself, and decides that 'he had taken up the wrong emotion for a Christian young man'. (p. 39).

(ii)   The other scene is that where Sue buys the statues of Apollo and Venus and hides them in her room, where Miss Fontover later finds and breaks them. She reflects on how strange they look, 'in odd contrast to their environment of text and martyr' (p. 103), especially as they happen to be standing on each side of a picture of the Crucifixion. This inspires her to read Gibbon's chapter about the reign of Julian the Apostate (the fourth-century Roman emperor who tried to revive the old Gods in place of Christianity) and also Swinburne's anti-Christian poem:

> Thou hast conquered, O pale Galilean;
> The world has grown grey from thy breath!

On the basis of what has been said so far, what do you think is Hardy's attitude to the Greeks, and to contemporary Christianity?

Discussion

Hardy seems to feel that Greek civilization stands for freedom and joyousness. The statue incident suggests that it also stands for uninhibited sexuality (Sue, you remember, is embarrassed after she has bought the figures because they are 'so very naked'). By contrast, Christianity is identified with repression. This doesn't just refer to Miss Fontover's petty persecution of Sue but is much more general; the pale figure of Christ on the cross seems to the girl to be turning the whole world grey.

Later on we hear Sue reciting some more profane poetry—'O ghastly glories of saints, dead limbs of gibbeted Gods!' (p. 157) which upsets Jude very much. This suggests that Christminster religion, with its emphasis on martrydom and the Crucifixion, means, for her, the glorification of suffering. And it is certainly true that orthodox Victorian Christianity did mean resisting certain natural feelings. Jude knows perfectly well that as one who hopes to become a clergyman he ought to keep away from Sue, because he is married. But he can't do it, and in the end he burns his books rather than leave her, 'I'll never care about my doctrines or my religion any more!' (p. 224). Sue says that she wants to 'make a virtue of joy . . . it was Nature's intention . . that we should be joyful in what instincts she afforded us—instincts which civilisation had taken upon itself to thwart' (p. 350).

So Hardy explicitly contrasts the Christian ethic of renunciation with the idea of following where one's instincts lead. But it would be a mistake to think that this always brings happiness. Phillotson makes himself bitterly unhappy by giving up Sue, under the influence of a strong inner prompting but in defiance of orthodox religion. And when Sue says that 'we have returned to Greek joyousness, and have blinded ourselves to sickness and suffering', I think Hardy's use of the phrase 'blinded ourselves' is significant, and that he means us to see her as blinding herself to *facts*.

All the four main characters in the novel have a complicated relationship with Christianity. Arabella is about the least religious person one can imagine, yet she becomes a convert for a short time after her husband dies and only gives it up when she becomes aware that 'after all that's said about the comforts of this religion, I wish I had Jude back again!' (p. 362). Phillotson, who has hoped to be a clergyman or at least a licentiate in the Church, makes this impossible for himself by his strange and—to most people—shocking action in tolerating Sue's going to live with her lover:

No man had ever suffered more inconvenience from his own charity, Christian or heathen, than Phillotson had done in letting Sue go. He had been knocked about from pillar to post at the hands of the virtuous almost beyond endurance; he had been nearly starved, and was now dependent entirely upon the very small stipend from the school of this village (where the parson had got ill-spoken of for befriending him) . . . Yet such was his obstinate and illogical disregard of opinion, and of the principles in which he had been trained, that his convictions on the rightness of his course with his wife had not been disturbed.
(p. 370)

But after the children's suicide Phillotson decides that he wants to go back to respectable life, and plays on Sue's feelings to make her come back to him:

'She's affected by Christminster sentiment and teaching. I can see her views on the indissolubility of marriage well enough, and I know where she got them. They are not mine, but I shall make use of them to further mine.'
(p. 371)

In what ways is Sue 'affected by Christminster sentiment and teaching? What has Christminster to do with her changed views about marriage?

Discussion

Sue has worked at Miss Fontover's shop and gone to services with her, although in those days she had no real religious beliefs. It's not clear why she should have done so, unless Christminster Anglicanism had an attraction for one part of her personality which she didn't admit. In fact she says, 'At times one couldn't help having a sneaking liking for the traditions of the old faith' (p. 157).

You shouldn't have had too much difficulty with my second question if you remembered what I said about the Oxford Movement earlier. After her children die, Sue feels an overwhelming sense of guilt and falls back on the religion of Christminster which tells her that she committed a sin in leaving her husband. It's natural, of course, that she should break down, but this breakdown might not have taken a religious form if she had not been so strongly influenced by Christminster traditions. When the gospel of joy can no longer help her, the Church (with its dogma of indissoluble marriage) is the obvious refuge. 'We should mortify the flesh,' she insists, 'the terrible flesh!' (p. 356). So we find her lying on the cold stone in front of the crucifix, ripping up her embroidered nightdress and ultimately forcing herself into Phillotson's bed, all of it in the name of religion.

At the beginning of the story Sue is a sceptic, while Jude is a believing Christian. At first he dreams of being a bishop, later he feels that:

To enter the Church in such an unscholarly way that he could not in any probability rise to a higher grade through all his career than that of the humble curate wearing his life out in an obscure village or city slum—that might have a touch of goodness and greatness in it; that might be true religion.

(p. 135)

Although he later comes to hate the Church for what it has done to Sue, when they have 'changed places' intellectually, he shows the same feelings about 'true religion' in what is almost his last conversation with her:

'Remember that the best and greatest among mankind are those who do themselves no worldly good. Every successful man is more or less a selfish man. The devoted fail. . . . "Charity seeketh not her own".'

'In that chapter we are at one, ever beloved darling, and on it we'll part friends. Its verses will stand fast when all the rest that you call religion has passed away!'

(p. 374)

Out of these four characters whose religious attitudes do you think are closest to Hardy's own?

Discussion

I think Hardy's views are definitely closest to Jude's (though I wouldn't disagree with you if you mentioned his sympathy for Phillotson in his lonely and unpopular struggle to do what he feels is right). But I think there can be no doubt that he identified with Jude much more deeply than with any other character, and Jude's career seems to mirror at least some of the struggles which Hardy went through as a young man. Like him, Jude thinks about going into the Church, loses his faith by imperceptible degrees and finally turns against organized religion. By the time he wrote his novel Hardy had become very bitter about large sections of the Established Church which seemed to him either smug or neurotic, and in any case quite indifferent to ordinary human problems (like the two clergymen whom he shows on page 349 arguing about the position of altars just after the children have died). We can hardly doubt his feeling that Sue had destroyed herself through her religious mania (look at the last paragraph of the novel) and any group, like the Oxford Movement, which seemed to put dogma above human beings made him angry, contemptuous and sarcastic. But, like Jude, he felt that the teaching of love was the essence of Christianity, and would survive after the dogmas had disappeared. For this reason he thought that Phillotson's giving Sue her freedom, though it is denounced by the Church, is an act of real love. But sticking too closely to the rules destroyed the very things that religion was supposed to be all about—'The letter killeth'.

4 MARRIAGE

One of the early reviews of *Jude*—not one of those I've quoted—was called, 'The Anti-Marriage League', and Hardy was persistently accused of trying to undermine marriage. It would be as well to get our facts clear from the start, so I would like you to find, if you can, a passage in which Hardy (not one of his characters) says clearly what he thinks on the subject of marriage and divorce.

Discussion

The passage I was thinking of comes from the 1912 Postscript, where Hardy wrote:

My opinion at that time, if I remember rightly, was what it is now, that a marriage should be dissoluble as soon as it becomes a cruelty to either of the parties—being then essentially and morally no marriage.

This seems to suggest that Hardy didn't particularly respect marriage as a legal bond, but did value the 'essential and moral' union between people. Now turn to Section 6, p. 49 and look at his first letter to Edmund Gosse. You'll see that he says there that he was not attempting to discuss 'the *general* marriage question', but to study 'the tragic issues of two bad marriages, owing in the main to a doom or curse of hereditary temperament peculiar to the family of the parties'. The problem of heredity, though Hardy doesn't explore it as fully as he might have, is a very important part of the background of the novel. Jude's aunt tells him several times that the Fawleys ought not to marry at all, let alone marry each other, and the union between Jude and Sue means 'a terrible intensification of unfitness—two bitters in one dish' (p. 176).

Part of the reason is that these particular people dislike being forced in any way:

'The men and women of our family are very generous when everything depends upon their good-will, but they always kick against compulsion. Don't you dread the attitude that insensibly arises out of legal obligation? Don't you think it is destructive to a passion whose essence is its gratuitousness?'

(p. 281)

Does this remind you of anything we discussed in Section 3 on Religion?

34

Discussion

I think Hardy is making the same general criticism of marriage as he did of orthodox Christianity. If society (or the Church) insists that marriage is a contract which must be kept however people happen to feel about it, then there is a danger that love will fly out of the window. 'The letter killeth', as Hardy said on the title-page. He expresses this idea several times through comparing a bad marriage to a trap which contorts and imprisons people. This is Jude's state of mind after he realizes that he should never have married Arabella:

He was inclined to inquire what he had done . . . that he deserved to be caught in a gin which would cripple him, if not her also, for the rest of a lifetime?   (p. 68)

In another place he says that people live under 'an artificial system of things', in which 'the normal sex-impulses are turned into devilish domestic gins and springes to noose and hold back those who want to progress (p. 226). There is one scene where Hardy shows us an actual example of a creature caught in a trap. Can you remember which?

Discussion

The scene (pages 222–4) when the rabbit is caught in a steel trap, from which it can't escape without being mutilated, so that the only kindness is to kill it. It follows naturally, in the pattern of the novel, that just after Jude has put the rabbit out of its misery he should see Sue, who tells him that she is miserable married to Phillotson. Immediately after this, when she goes back to her husband, Hardy shows us her frantic struggles to escape from a situation which is real torture to her. If you look back at the Introduction you'll remember that I pointed out various places where Hardy uses the image of people being forced into 'moulds' which do not fit them, and concludes from this that there is something radically wrong with society—he doesn't say what. (But what is wrong, incidentally, is *not* the divorce laws, for neither Jude nor Sue have any trouble with the actual mechanics of getting divorced.)

Hardy shows two marriages which have gone wrong in this novel. Can you say as briefly as possible what is the matter with Jude's marriage to Arabella, and Phillotson's to Sue?

My Answers

Jude has nothing mentally in common with Arabella, and only sexual attraction draws them together (symbolically, she prevents him from going to Christminster, and flings his books on the floor). Sue likes Phillotson as a friend, but cannot bear their sexual relationship. So the two marriages have broken down in opposite ways.

In this context, you may remember that I pointed to Hardy's description of *Jude* as the story of 'a deadly war waged between flesh and spirit' as the most

35

important clue we have to the novel's meaning. Of course, this partly means the struggle between sexual and religious feelings, which we talked about in Section 3, but it has a wider meaning too. 'The spirit' can mean a whole range of different things, and 'the flesh' doesn't only mean sex. To make clearer what I mean by this, I'd like you to re-read the scene (pages 202–4) where Jude goes to see the musician whose work has affected him so deeply. Does this have any relevance to Hardy's purpose of showing the war between spirit and flesh?

Discussion

Hardy shows us a man who has just written a beautiful and moving hymn about the Crucifixion, but who is giving up music because it doesn't pay (he's going into the wine trade, and is only interested in Jude as a potential customer). He has become what the Victorians would have called 'worldly'—chiefly caring about money, and with no sense of spiritual values. Hardy tells us, incidentally, that 'he was brought up and educated in Christminster traditions, which accounts for the quality of the piece' (p. 202). But Jude has the disillusionment of finding out that, like Christminster and its religion, the musician appears to have spiritual depths which aren't really there. Nothing to do with sex, all this, but it's very relevant to Hardy's theme because it shows a man who has become obsessed with 'the fleshpots', and is denying the best part of his own nature.

This is only one example of the spirit and the flesh having got into a wrong relationship. Others I can think of are:

(i)   Jude taking Arabella out when he meant to spend the afternoon studying.

(ii)   Jude having to start thinking about 'the mean bread-and-cheese question' the morning after he gets to Christminster.

(iii)   Jude reciting the Latin Creed in a pub for a bet.

(iv)   Sue forcing herself to sleep with Phillotson.

Do you think that, in these four situations, the flesh is dominating the spirit or vice versa? You'll find my answers at the end of this Section, p. 39.

I hope I've said enough to convince you that the 'deadly war between flesh and spirit' takes place, in this novel, on many different levels. Hardy's irony helps to show us how very complex and all-embracing this 'deadly war' is; Christminster is an ethereal city which 'keeps ever calling us to the true goal of all of us, to the ideal, to perfection', but it's only open to those who can buy their way in, and it's also a place where 'there's wenches in the streets o' nights' and where the people hang round in low pubs. Jude wants to be a bishop and a scholar, but finds himself getting Arabella into trouble and slaughtering pigs. It's 'all contrasts'. Perhaps the most striking contrast of them all is between the two women, Arabella and Sue, in whom the qualities of 'flesh' and 'spirit' are almost personified. Consider the difference between these two voices:

(i)

Arabella replied in a curiously low, hungry tone of latent sensuousness; 'I've got him to care for me: yes! But I want him to more than care for me; I want him to have me—to marry me. I must have him. I can't do without him. He's the sort of man I long for. I shall go mad if I can't give myself to him altogether! I felt I should when I first saw him!' (p. 55)

(ii)

She added in hurt tones, without turning round, 'My liking for you is not as some women's perhaps. But it is a delight in being with you, of a supremely delicate kind, and I don't want to go further and risk it by—an attempt to intensify it!' (p. 250)

I think these two extracts illuminate the difference between them far better than any words of mine could do. Arabella is aggressively sexual ('She is such a low-passioned woman,' Sue says disapprovingly, 'I can see it in her shape!' (p. 273), whereas Sue is 'hardly flesh at all' (p. 255) 'so ethereal a creature that her spirit could be seen trembling through her limbs' (p. 195). You remember that in the Section on Hardy's method we looked at the imagery which he uses to describe the two women and noticed the same kind of flesh/ spirit contrast. In the beginning Jude tries to think of Sue in completely 'spiritual' terms, as 'a kindly star, an elevating power, a companion in Anglican worship, a tender friend' (p. 97). But of course this breaks down, because what he is really looking for is a woman with whom he can have a complete physical and emotional relationship, and this is precisely what Sue cannot give. It's not a question of a contrast between a 'good' woman and a 'bad' one who offer respectively a good and a bad marriage;[1] the trouble is that both women can only offer a limited relationship to Jude:

One point illustrating this I could not dwell upon, that, though she has children, her intimacies with Jude have never been more than occasional, even when they were living together (I mention that they occupy separate rooms, except towards the end) and one of her reasons for fearing the marriage ceremony is that she fears it would be breaking faith with Jude to withhold herself at pleasure, or altogether, after it; though while uncontracted she feels at liberty to yield herself as seldom as she chooses. This has tended to keep his passion as hot at the end as at the beginning, and helps to break his heart. He has never really possessed her as freely as he desired.

Thus Hardy wrote to Edmund Gosse after the novel was published (the reason, of course, why he 'could not dwell upon' this point was the prudishness of the Victorian public). Clearly, this novel is more than a manifesto against the marriage laws, and one of the prime reasons for Jude's failure and tragedy is the nature of Sue.

I want to talk a bit more about this complex and fascinating character because, if we don't understand her, the novel hardly makes sense. We know from Hardy's own words, if it isn't obvious, that she is 'a type of woman which has always had an attraction for me'. He talks about her 'indefinable charm' (p. 378) and I think most readers feel this, although if we only looked at what she actually does we might be tempted to call her a bitch. Gillingham, Phillotson's

---

[1] This contrast was very common in the nineteenth-century novel, like that between the 'pure' Fanny and the 'corrupt' Mary Crawford, or the unworldly Dorothea and the calculating Rosamond.

friend, describes her as 'a little hussy' because, like most normal people, he can't understand her behaviour. This is after she has come back to see Phillotson when she has made him ill—'She just came, patted my pillow with her little white hand, played the thoughtful nurse for half an hour, and went away' (p. 263). Before this she has lived with a Christminster undergraduate but refused to be his mistress; significantly, he dies. Afterwards she tries to live on the same terms with Jude, and it could be said that in the end she kills him by leaving him. Jude certainly intends to kill himself when he goes to see her for the last time in the rain. 'Well, I'm blest! Kill yourself for a woman!' (p. 405) is the outraged reaction of Arabella.

Sue does do harm to nearly everyone she gets involved with—the undergraduate, Phillotson, Jude, her children (as I want to argue in the next Section). Yet the indefinable charm remains, and I think that we can't read the novel without being aware of a frighteningly deep and painful emotion among all the irony with which Hardy writes about Sue. This is one reason why I personally find it difficult not to believe that Sue's character was inspired by an actual woman he had known. And this is why we don't find it incredible that Jude, although he knows to his cost exactly how contradictory, demanding and perverse she can be, keeps on loving her, in spite of all this, till he dies.

Look back at the first scene (pages 99–103) in which we meet Sue directly. We've studied this before, and I mentioned then that it gave me the impression of a girl who is literally terrified of deep commitments. She seems to be very independent intellectually (or she wouldn't be questioning the Christianity of her environment) *and* very dependent emotionally (or she wouldn't keep her views a secret; she can't even face having a showdown with Miss Fontover apparently).

The same pattern can be traced in her relationships with the various men in her life. She will flirt with them, share a house with them, even marry them sometimes, but the one thing she doesn't want is complete involvement. But she does have a conscience, and when she has gone to the one extreme of being a heartless flirt she will impulsively rush to the other extreme to compensate. As Jude puts it, rather brutally, about her treatment of Phillotson, 'You simply mean that you flirted outrageously with him, poor old chap, and then repented, and to make reparation, married him, though you tortured yourself to death by doing it' (p. 252).

It is Sue's penchant for self-torture, disguised as Christian mortification of the flesh,[1] which, in the end, destroys her. And I think that the fact that she destroys herself, as well as other people, is one reason why it is impossible for Hardy to blame her. He calls her 'a scared child' (p. 179), a 'poor little bird' (p. 219), and a 'poor little quivering thing' (p. 380). 'Chastened, world-weary, remorseful, the strain on her nerves had preyed upon her flesh and bones' (p. 381) he says when Sue marries Phillotson for the second time, and his final word is that she will never find peace again 'till she's as he [Jude] is now' (p. 423).

Not surprisingly, the Victorian critics didn't know what to make of Sue, as no heroine quite like her had ever appeared in literature before, and it was left to a German reviewer to tell Hardy:

Sue Bridehead, the heroine, was the first delineation in fiction of the woman who was coming into notice in her thousands every year—the woman of the feminist movement—the slight, pale 'bachelor' girl—the intellectualised,

---

[1] The Oxford Movement revived many practices like celibacy, fasting and scourging oneself.

emancipated bundle of nerves that modern conditions were producing, mainly in cities as yet; who does not recognise the necessity for most of her sex to follow marriage as a profession. . . .   (1912 Postscript)

This is a thought-provoking description, and one which makes the novel sound even more 'modern' than the Victorians thought it was. But I don't think that Hardy meant Sue to represent the typical woman of the future, though he certainly did feel that the role of women in modern society must be radically questioned. On the contrary, he seems to have felt that it is only the rare woman, like Sue, who cannot adjust to marriage, and that it is only social and external pressures which force her into relationships with men. 'You were a distinct type,' Jude says, 'a refined creature, intended by Nature to be left intact' (p. 355), and a little later he asserts, 'Yours is not a passionate heart . . . you are, upon the whole, a sort of fay, or sprite—not a woman' (p. 365). D. H. Lawrence, in a fascinating essay on *Jude*,[1] came to very much the same conclusion, 'She was no woman', and he felt that because of this the relationship was never valid anyway:

Sue and Jude could not lie to themselves, in their last and deepest feelings. They knew it was no marriage, they knew it was wrong, all along; they knew they were sinning against life, in forcing a physical marriage between themselves. . . . The real marriage of Jude and Sue was in the roses.

My answers to the exercise on p. 36

In the first three examples the flesh is dominating the spirit. In the fourth one the spirit is dominating the flesh.

5   HARDY'S PESSIMISM

Most readers seem to think that Hardy was a 'pessimist'—whatever that means!—and that *Jude* is the most 'pessimistic' of all his novels. (This view has been argued in the radio talk by David Lodge, with which I don't altogether agree.) Before going any further, it might be as well to make quite sure what the word 'pessimist' means. The *Shorter Oxford English Dictionary* defines a pessimist as:

(a)   One who habitually takes the worst view of things, and

(b)   one who holds the metaphysical doctrine of pessimism.

'Pessimism' is defined as:

(a)   The tendency to look at the worst aspect of things, and

(b)   the doctrine that this world is the worst possible, or that everything naturally tends to evil.

Hardy was sensitive to accusations of pessimism. He commented in 1922, when he was over eighty:

---

[1] *Thomas Hardy*, in *Phoenix* reprinted in A. Beal (ed.), *D. H. Lawrence: Selected Literary Criticism*, Heinemann Educational 1967. This essay is much too long for me to quote, but I do urge you to read it if you can and see whether you agree with it.

If I may be forgiven for quoting my own old words, let me repeat what I printed in this relation more than twenty years ago, and wrote much earlier, in a poem entitled *In Tenebris*:

'If way to the Better there be, it exacts a full look at the Worst.'

. . . Comment on where the world stands is very much the reverse of needless in these disordered years of our prematurely afflicted century . . . amendment and not madness lies that way.[1]

Do you think, on the basis of Hardy's own words, that he is a pessimist in sense (a) or sense (b) or both? Think about this carefully and note down your conclusions.

My Answers

I think that Hardy certainly is a pessimist in the sense that he 'looks at the worst aspect of things' (which isn't quite the same, when you think about it, as 'habitually taking the worst view of things'). But judging by the words I've just quoted he does *not* seem to think that 'this world is the worst possible, or that everything naturally tends to evil'. On the contrary, he's saying that there is every chance that the world can be made better, if human beings are only prepared to look at their problems in a realistic way.

Hardy was always hurt by the charge that he made things blacker than they really were, because he felt that all he had done was to 'comment on where the world stood'. Many things in *Jude* which would once have been called 'pessimistic' or 'cynical' would only be described as 'realistic' today. Victorian readers, by and large, wanted their novels to end on a note of reassurance (you remember how Dickens changed the ending of *Great Expectations* because his friends thought that the public would be upset). Many novels of the time showed the hero or heroine making an unhappy marriage, but they usually solved the problem by killing off the unsuitable husband or wife. Hardy had done this himself in his earlier novels, but he recognizes in *Jude* that things don't usually work so conveniently. Again, it's inevitable that Jude's dream of becoming a student at Christminster should fail. It was impossible for a working man to go to Oxford at the time the novel was written, and Hardy would have been falsifying the facts if he had made him succeed.

But what about the episode which has done more than anything else to prejudice people against the novel—the scene in which Little Father Time hangs his brother and sister and himself? This is definitely *not* the kind of thing that happens in the ordinary course of events, and many readers, both then and now, felt that Hardy was loading the dice against his characters, creating a completely incredible situation just because he wanted to make them suffer. A contemporary reviewer summed up the objections against the scene in these words:

Now, up to this point, woe has been heaped upon woe, and the reader has accepted it all, with some reservations, as a natural evolution of the circumstances. The tragedy of the children strains his belief to snapping point; and then comes a perfectly superfluous touch which snaps it altogether. Jude reports to the suffering mother of two of the dead little ones the opinion of the doctor,

---

[1] From the Preface to *Late Lyrics and Earlier*, in Hardy's *Collected Poems*.

who, oddly enough, happens to be 'an advanced man'. He is so 'advanced' as to assure the father that unnatural children who murder their brothers and commit suicide are becoming common, owing to the 'universal wish not to live'. This is too much. Fortunately, it comes so near the end that the extraordinary power and even beauty of the book are not destroyed; but it is strange that Mr Hardy did not perceive how he had imperilled the whole fabric by a stroke which passes the border of burlesque. The horror of the infant pessimist is changed in a moment to ghastly farce by this inopportune generalisation of the 'advanced' doctor. We all know perfectly well that baby Schopenhauers are not coming into the world in shoals. Children whose lives, stunted by poverty or disease, have acquired a gravity beyond their years, may be found everywhere in the overcrowded centres of population; but such a portrait as little Jude Fawley, who advocates the annihilation of the species, and gives a practical example of it at an early age, does not present itself as typical of a devouring philosophy.[1]

This seems a good summary of the case against the novel as Hardy wrote it, and if you agree, you would have to say that *Jude* is seriously flawed. But I think it is worth looking at this episode in some detail, to see how it fits into the whole novel, and perhaps then you can decide whether or not Hardy made a mistake.

To begin with I'd like you to consider these questions:

(i)   What is little Jude's heredity?

(ii)   What has his early life been like?

(iii)   What kind of life has his family been leading over the last few years?

(iv)   What happens to them on their first day in Christminster?

My Answers

(i)   Little Jude, like his father, is the child of a broken marriage, and on the Fawley side he comes from a 'cross-grained, unfortunate, almost accursed stock' (p. 97). We know from Hardy's first letter to Edmund Gosse that he intended 'the tragic issues of two bad marriages' to be one of the novel's major themes. Jude fears, when he first becomes involved with Sue, that

even were he free, in a family like his own where marriage usually meant a tragic sadness, marriage with a blood-relation would duplicate the adverse conditions, and a tragic sadness might be intensified to a tragic horror.

(p. 97)

Of course, the little boy was not born from the union between Jude and Sue, but it does—Hardy feels—affect him in a different way:

The boy's face expressed the whole tale of their situation. On that little shape had converged all the inauspiciousness and shadow which had darkened the first union of Jude, and all the accidents, mistakes, fears, errors of the last. He was their nodal point, their focus, their expression in a single term. For the rashness of those parents he had groaned, for their ill-assortment he had quaked, and for the misfortunes of these he had died.   (p. 348)

---

[1] Review in *Illustrated London News*, quoted in *Thomas Hardy and his Readers op. cit.*, p. 125.

41

I take this as meaning that he was the victim, first of a bad heredity (a subject which, as we've seen, Hardy took seriously) and then of the 'accidents, mistakes, fears, errors . . . misfortunes' which have dogged Jude and Sue.

(ii)   He has spent his early life in Australia with Arabella's parents, who didn't have him christened 'because, if I died in damnation, 'twould save the expense of a Christian funeral' (p. 289). Neither they nor his mother wanted to have him with them.

(iii)   Over the last few years the boy's adoptive parents have been constantly moving about, because they can't face the gossip about their marital status, and getting poorer and poorer.

(iv)   Arriving at Christminster (which strikes the little boy as a very sinister place) they get caught in the rain and have to trail about to look for lodgings. The majority of people 'don't let where there are children' (p. 341). When they do find rooms Sue admits to the landlady that she is not married and they are asked to leave. They look for another lodging but can't find one.

I want you now to read pages 343–5 very carefully, from 'The failure to find another lodging . . .' to '. . . go to sleep!' What do you think of Sue's way of talking to the child?

Discussion

I think the strongest feeling that comes over is of Sue's dreadful irresponsibility in taking out her depression on the child. To tell him that 'all is trouble, adversity and suffering', and to agree limply ('It would almost, dear') when he asks her if they wouldn't be better dead, is helping to drive him frantic. She then blurts out that she is going to have another baby (just as she has earlier blurted out to the landlady that she is not married) and this is the last straw. What happens afterwards is largely because of this—'her discourse with the boy had been the main cause of the tragedy' (p. 347). This doesn't just show up Sue's ineptitude in ordinary human affairs. I think Hardy is also showing us that Sue is lacking in most of the normal human instincts, including the instincts of a mother. ('She was glad to have children', D. H. Lawrence wrote, 'to prove she was a woman. But in her it was a perversity to wish to prove she was a woman. She was no woman.'[1])

You may or may not feel that it was a mistake for Hardy to have written this episode. But it seems that Hardy himself thought it was central to his novel (we can see him preparing for it, a long way back, when he writes things like 'a tragic sadness might be intensified to a tragic horror'). And when we look at the number of pressures on the child—his heredity and background; Sue's incompetence; the family's destitution—it does seem more convincing than it did at first that, in that particular situation, he should be driven into doing something desperate. But Hardy is also raising a wider issue:

'The doctor says there are such boys springing up amongst us—boys of a sort unknown in the last generation—the outcome of new views of life. They seem to see all its terrors before they are old enough to have staying power to resist them. He says it is the beginning of the coming universal wish not to live'.

(p. 348)

---

[1] *Thomas Hardy*, printed in *Phoenix*, *op. cit.*

You remember that the reviewer I quoted ridiculed this, 'We all know that baby Schopenhauers are not coming into the world in shoals'. But in the next sentence he went on to say, 'Children whose lives, stunted by poverty or disease, have acquired a gravity beyond their years, may be found everywhere in the over-crowded centres of population'. And this, I believe, is the heart of the problem which Hardy is trying to explore.

Hardy isn't merely saying that an exceptional child in exceptional circumstances might do what Little Father Time does, though he thinks it perfectly credible that this should happen. He also seems to have a vague, but deep feeling that this foreshadows a great disaster which may be in store for the next generation, though he couldn't have said what he meant more precisely than that. Little Father Time isn't an *average* child in the sense that other children behave in exactly the same way, but Hardy did feel that he might be a *typical* child, in the sense that he represents certain forces which might tear the whole of society apart.[1] The situation of Jude and Sue hunting for work and lodgings is certainly typical; the average Victorian working-class family with its eight or nine children was involved in exactly the same kind of struggle for life. In his last two novels, Hardy seems to have been haunted by the fate of these children. In *Tess of the D'Urbervilles* he shows a girl being forced to live with a man she hates because her little brothers and sisters will starve if she doesn't (and it's worth reminding ourselves that children starved to death in England less than eighty years ago). In *Jude*, he doesn't state the problem in such specific terms, but it's still there in the background. 'It seems such a terribly tragic thing', says Sue, 'to bring beings into the world' (p. 322). Dickens probably wrote more than any other great novelist about these children whose lives had been 'stunted by poverty or disease', and he seems to have shared Hardy's fears for them. One of the most striking examples of this can be found in *A Christmas Carol*, where the Spirit shows Scrooge a couple of horrifying little waifs and tells him:

'This boy is Ignorance; this girl is Want. Beware them both . . . but most of all beware this boy, for I see that written on his brow which is Doom, if the writing be not erased.'[2]

Dickens is using an essentially *poetic* image here, to express his very real fears about the future of England, and I think that we can best understand Hardy's parable of the children's death if we see that, too, as a poetic expression of his feelings. Although he isn't usually compared with Dickens, their minds often worked in very much the same way.

Is it not fair, then, to call Hardy a pessimist, if his vision of the future was so tragic? I think Hardy would have said that this was a *possible* future to which we must not blind ourselves, 'If way to the Better there be, it exacts a full look at the Worst'. (The worst, when it came, was considerably worse than Hardy could have imagined. The Great War, which Hardy said destroyed his belief in progress, started less than twenty years after *Jude* came out).

But although the novel ends tragically for most of the characters, this doesn't mean that Hardy felt life was tragic always and everywhere. There are degrees in these things, and Sue's breakdown is a worse tragedy than Jude's death (he reproaches her, 'I *would* have died game!' (p. 403)). Even at the end, Jude

---

[1] Other nineteenth-century novelists, like Stendhal and Dostoevsky, treated crimes of this sort seriously, as revealing some deep trend or problem within the society they were depicting.

[2] *A Christmas Carol*, Stave 3.

goes on believing in the future, 'I hear that soon there is going to be a better chance for such helpless students as I was. . . . Our ideas were fifty years too soon. . . .' (pp. 413–14).

Is the final impression of the novel one of hopelessness and despair? I don't think so. There is something almost jubilant about the last chapter in the book, with its lively description of the carnival at Christminster, and the 'pink and blue and yellow ladies', and the crowds of workers going to watch the boat-race (this is the first time that Hardy has ever shown Christminster as a place where ordinary people enjoy themselves). A bitter contrast, perhaps, with the lonely death of Jude. But that last section of all gives me the distinct impression that, if Sue has been defeated, Jude has not—or, at any rate, not quite:

Two days later, when the sky was equally cloudless, and the air equally still, two persons stood beside Jude's open coffin in the same little bedroom. On one side was Arabella, on the other the Widow Edlin. They were both looking at Jude's face, the worn old eyelids of Mrs Edlin being red.

'How beautiful he is!' said she.

'Yes. He's a 'andsome corpse,' said Arabella.

. . . An occasional word, as from someone making a speech, floated from the open windows of the Theatre across to this quiet corner, at which there seemed to be a smile of some sort upon the marble features of Jude; while the old, superseded, Delphin editions of Virgil and Horace, and the dog-eared Greek Testament on the neighbouring shelf, and the few other volumes of the sort that he had not parted with, roughened with stone-dust where he had been in the habit of catching them up for a few minutes between his labours, seemed to pale to a sickly cast at the sounds. The bells struck out joyously, and their reverberations travelled round the bedroom.

(p. 422)

Crowd on Magdalene Bridge, Oxford, listening to May Morning singing 1895 (Taunt Collection, Oxford City Libraries)

6   SOME CRITICAL OPINIONS

If you want to read more about Hardy, one of the best works is Douglas Brown's *Thomas Hardy*, Macmillan, 1954, although this doesn't say very much about *Jude*. The whole question of Hardy's 'pessimism' is re-argued in an interesting book by Roy Morrell, *Thomas Hardy: The Will and the Way*, Oxford University Press, 1956. Best of all for beginners is F. B. Pinion's *A Hardy Companion*, Macmillan, 1968.

If you would like to read a really stimulating commentary on *Jude*, do get hold of D. H. Lawrence's essay 'Thomas Hardy', which is in *Phoenix*, and read the section relating to the novel. But remember that Lawrence is an eccentric writer, and that sometimes he seems to be thinking how much better a novel *Jude* would have been, if he had written it himself!

Finally, I'm giving you a selection from the first reviews of the novel, all of which are published along with others in *Thomas Hardy and his Readers*, by Laurence Lerner and John Holmstrom, Bodley Head, 1968. Among them are two short letters from Hardy to Edmund Gosse, which you should read very carefully, and which I've quoted for discussion in this Unit.

The World, 13 November 1895

Hardy the Degenerate

Not many weeks ago the announcement that Mr. Thomas Hardy's new novel, in the course of its passage through the pages of *Harper's Magazine*, had been condensed and modified in the alleged interests of propriety moved us to utter a protest against the excesses of this bowdlerising spirit. We are reluctantly compelled to admit, now that *Jude the Obscure* (Osgood, McIlvaine) is published 'as originally written,' that the editor of the magazine in question cannot in any fairness be convicted of excessive 'pandering to Podsnap.' What he did in the main was to relieve Mr. Hardy's pages of realistic details which are not merely gratuitous, but disgusting. *Jude the Obscure*, says Mr. Hardy, is a novel 'addressed by a man to men and women of full age,' and, that being so, he holds himself exempted from the necessity of 'mincing' his words. Granted: but that is no excuse for demanding of his reader the gastric imperturbability of a well-seasoned pork-butcher. The opening scene of Jude's courtship of Arabella—we beg pardon, of Arabella's courtship of Jude—is enough to sicken a scavenger. As for the nauseating chapter devoted to the killing of the pig, it may best be described as an act of literary suicide. Perhaps, as the novel was primarily destined for an American audience, all this talk of chitterlings and 'innerds' was meant as a delicate compliment to the inhabitants of Porkopolis, Ohio. But we doubt whether the average full-grown British man or woman cares sufficiently for wading in pigstyes or shambles to appreciate Mr. Hardy's graphic and circumstantial delineation of the last hours and butchering of the obscure one's fatted porker. We are not so sure, however, that Mr. Hardy's Wessex peasants, especially that 'complete and substantial female human,' as he elegantly describes Jude's first sweetheart, are not even more swinish in their ways than his pigs. The frank animalism of Arabella's methods makes one almost regret the disappearance of the porcine *dramatis personæ* so early in the story. A pig, at any rate, if it makes no pretence to lead the higher life, is at least never morbid. And, so far as we are aware, there are no New or Obscure Pigs even in the kingdom of Wessex.

. . . Mr. Hardy, in short, seems to have become equally enamoured of the methods of Zola and Tolstoi—Zola of *La Terre*, and Tolstoi the decadent sociologist. It is a bad blend, and the results, as manifested in the volume before us, are anything but satisfactory. Humanity, as envisaged by Mr. Hardy, is largely compounded of hoggishness and hysteria. . . .

Cosmopolis, January 1896

. . . It is a study of four lives, a rectangular problem in failures, drawn with almost mathematical rigidity. The tragedy of these four persons is constructed in a mode almost as geometrical as that in which Dr. Samuel Clarke was wont to prove the existence of the Deity. It is difficult not to believe that the author set up his four ninepins in the wilds of Wessex, and built up his theorem round them. Here is an initial difficulty. Not quite thus is theology or poetry conveniently composed; we like to conceive that the relation of the parts was more spontaneous, we like to feel that the persons of a story have been thrown up in a jet of enthusiasm, not put into a cave of theory to be slowly covered with stalactite.

'Jude the Obscure' is acted in North Wessex (Berkshire) and just across the frontier, at Christminster (Oxford), which is not in Wessex at all. We want our novelist back among the rich orchards of the Hintocks, and where the water-lilies impede the lingering river at Shottsford Ash. Berkshire is an unpoetical county, 'meanly utilitarian,' as Mr. Hardy confesses; the imagination hates its concave, loamy cornfields and dreary, hedgeless highways. The local history has been singularly tampered with in Berkshire; it is useless to speak to us of ancient records where the past is all obliterated, and the thatched and dormered houses replaced by modern cottages. In choosing North Wessex as the scene of a novel Mr. Hardy wilfully deprives himself of a great element of his strength. Where there are no prehistoric monuments, no ancient buildings, no mossed and immemorial woodlands, he is Samson shorn. In Berkshire, the change which is coming over England so rapidly, the resignation of the old dreamy elements of beauty, has proceeded further than anywhere else in Wessex. Pastoral loveliness is to be discovered only here and there, while in Dorsetshire it still remains the master-element. All this combines to lessen the physical charm of 'Jude the Obscure' to those who turn from it in memory to 'Far from the Madding Crowd' and 'The Return of the Native.'

But, this fortuitous absence of beauty being acknowledged, the novelist's hand shows no falling off in the vigour and reality of his description. It may be held, in fact, to be a lesser feat to raise before us an enchanting vision of the valley of the Froom, than successfully to rivet our attention on the prosaic arable land encircling the dull hamlet of Marygreen.

To pass from the landscape to the persons, two threads of action seem to be intertwined in 'Jude the Obscure.' We have, first of all, the contrast between the ideal life the young peasant of scholarly instincts wished to lead, and the squalid real life into which he was fated to sink. We have, secondly, the almost rectilinear puzzle of the sexual relations of the four principal characters. Mr. Hardy has wished to show how cruel destiny can be to the eternal dream of youth, and he has undertaken to trace the lamentable results of unions in a family exhausted by intermarriage and poverty. Some collision is apparent between these aims; the first seems to demand a poet, the second a physician. The Fawleys are a decayed and wasted race, in the last of whom, Jude, there appears, with a kind of flicker in the socket, a certain intellectual and artistic brightness. In favourable surroundings, we feel that this young man might have become fairly distinguished as a scholar, or as a sculptor. But at the supreme moment, or at each supreme moment, the conditions hurl him back into insignificance. When we examine clearly what these conditions are, we find them to be instinctive. He is just going to develop into a lad of education, when Arabella throws her hideous missile at him, and he sinks with her into a resigned inferiority.

So far, the critical court is with Mr. Hardy; these scenes and their results give a perfect impression of truth. Later on, it is not quite evident whether the claim on Jude's passions, or the inherent weakness of his inherited character, is the source of his failure. Perhaps both. But it is difficult to see what part Oxford has in his destruction, or how Mr. Hardy can excuse the rhetorical diatribes against the university which appear towards the close of the book. Does the novelist really think that it was the duty of the heads of houses to whom Jude wrote his crudely pathetic letters to offer him immediately a fellowship? We may admit to the full the pathos of Jude's position—nothing is more heart-rending than the obscurity of the half-educated—but surely, the fault did not lie with Oxford.

The scene at Commemoration (Part VI). is of a marvellous truth and vividness of presentment, but it would be stronger, and even more tragic, if Mr. Hardy did not appear in it as an advocate taking sides with his unhappy hero. In this portion of his work, it seems to me, Mr. Hardy had but to paint—as clearly and as truthfully as he could—the hopes, the struggles, the disappointments of Jude, and of these he has woven a tissue of sombre colouring, indeed, and even of harsh threads, but a tapestry worthy of a great imaginative writer. It was straightforward poet's work in invention and observation, and he has executed it well.

. . . It does not appear to me that we have any business to call in question the right of a novelist of Mr. Hardy's extreme distinction to treat what themes he will. We may wish—and I for my part cordially wish—that more pleasing, more charming plots than this could take his fancy. But I do not feel at liberty to challenge his discretion. One thing, however, the critic of comparative literature must note. We have, in such a book as 'Jude the Obscure,' traced the full circle of propriety. A hundred and fifty years ago, Fielding and Smollett brought up before us pictures, used expressions, described conduct, which appeared to their immediate successors a little more crude than general reading warranted. In Miss Burney's hands and in Miss Austin's, the morals were still further hedged about. Scott was even more daintily reserved. We came at last to Dickens, where the clamorous passions of mankind, the coarser accidents of life, were absolutely ignored, and the whole question of population seemed reduced to the theory of the gooseberry bush. This was the *ne plus ultra* of decency; Thackeray and George Eliot relaxed this intensity of prudishness; once on the turn, the tide flowed rapidly, and here is Mr. Hardy ready to say any mortal thing that Fielding said, and a good deal more too.

So much we note, but to censure it, if it calls for censure, is the duty of the moralist and not the critic. Criticism asks how the thing is done, whether the execution is fine and convincing. To tell so squalid and so abnormal a story in an interesting way is in itself a feat, and this, it must be universally admitted, Mr. Hardy has achieved. 'Jude the Obscure' is an irresistible book; it is one of those novels into which we descend and are carried on by a steady impetus to the close, when we return, dazzled, to the light of common day. The two women, in particular, are surely created by a master. Every impulse, every speech, which reveals to us the coarse and animal, but not hateful Arabella, adds to the solidity of her portrait. We may dislike her, we may hold her intrusion into our consciousness a disagreeable one, but of her reality there can be no question: Arabella lives.

It is conceivable that not so generally will it be admitted that Sue Bridehead is convincing. Arabella is the excess of vulgar normality; every public bar and village fair knows Arabella, but Sue is a strange and unwelcome product of exhaustion. The *vita sexualis* of Sue is the central interest of the book, and enough is told about it to fill the specimen tables of a German specialist. Fewer testimonies will be given to her reality than to Arabella's because hers is much the rarer case. But her picture is not less admirably drawn; Mr. Hardy has, perhaps, never devoted so much care to the portrait of a woman. She is a poor, maimed 'degenerate,' ignorant of herself and of the perversion of her instincts, full of febrile, amiable illusions, ready to dramatise her empty life, and play at loving though she cannot love. Her adventure with the undergraduate has not taught her what she is; she quits Phillotson still ignorant of the source of her repulsion; she lives with Jude, after a long, agonising struggle, in a relation that she accepts with distaste, and when the tragedy comes, and her children are killed, her poor extravagant brain slips one grade further down, and she sees in this calamity the chastisement of God. What has she done to be chastised? She does not know, but supposes it must be her abandonment of Phillotson, to whom, in a spasm of self-abasement, and shuddering with repulsion, she returns without a thought for the misery of Jude. It is a terrible study in pathology, but of the splendid success of it, of the sustained intellectual force implied in the evolution of it, there cannot, I think, be two opinions.

One word must be added about the speech of the author and of the characters in 'Jude the Obscure.' Is it too late to urge Mr. Hardy to struggle against the jarring note of rebellion which seems growing upon him? It sounded in 'Tess,' and here it is, more roughly expressed, further acerbated. What has Providence done to Mr. Hardy that he should rise up in the arable land of Wessex and shake his fist at his Creator? He should not force his talent, should not give way to these chimerical outbursts of philosophy falsely so called. His early romances were full of calm and lovely pantheism; he seemed in them to feel the deep-hued country landscapes full of rural gods, all homely and benign. We wish he would go back to Egdon Heath and listen to the singing in the heather. . . .

A fact about the infancy of Mr. Hardy has escaped the interviewers and may be recorded here. On the day of his birth, during a brief absence of his nurse, there slipped into the room an ethereal creature, known as the Spirit of Plastic Beauty. Bending over the cradle she scattered roses on it, and as she strewed them she blessed the babe. 'He shall have an eye to see moral and material loveliness, he shall speak of richly-coloured pastoral places in the accent of Theocritus, he shall write in such a way as to cajole busy men into a sympathy with old, unhappy, far-off things.' She turned and went, but while the nurse still delayed, a withered termagant glided into the room. From her apron she dropped toads among the rose-leaves, and she whispered: 'I am the genius of False Rhetoric, and led by me he shall say things ugly and coarse, not recognising them to be so, and shall get into a rage about matters that call for philosophic calm, and shall spoil some of his best passages with pedantry and incoherency. He shall not know what things belong to his peace, and he shall plague his most loyal admirers with the barbaric contortions of his dialogue.' So saying, she put out her snaky tongue at the unoffending babe, and ever since, his imagination, noble as it is, and attuned to the great harmonies of nature, is liable at a moment's notice to give a shriek of discord. The worst, however, which any honest critic can say of 'Jude the Obscure' is that the fairy godmother seems, for the moment, to have relaxed her guardianship a little unduly.

EDMUND GOSSE

Letter from Hardy to Edmund Gosse, 10 November 1895

> Max Gate
> Dorchester
> November 10th 1895

My Dear Gosse,

Your review is the most discriminating that has yet appeared. It required an artist to see that the plot is almost geometrically constructed—I ought not to say *constructed*, for, beyond a certain point, the characters necessitated it, and I simply let it come. As for the story itself, it is really sent out to those into whose souls the iron has entered, and has entered deeply at some time of their lives. But one cannot choose one's readers.

It is curious that some of the papers should look upon the novel as a manifesto on 'the marriage question' (although, of course, it involves it), seeing that it is concerned first with the labours of a poor student to get a University degree, and secondly with the tragic issues of two bad marriages, owing in the main to a doom or curse of hereditary temperament peculiar to the family of the parties. The only remarks which can be said to bear on the *general* marriage question occur in dialogue, and comprise no more than half a dozen pages in a book of five hundred. And of these remarks I state (p. 362) that my own views are not expressed therein. I suppose the attitude of these critics is to be accounted for by the accident that during the serial publication of my story, a sheaf of 'purpose' novels on the matter appeared.

You have hardly an idea how poor and feeble the book seems to me, as executed, beside the idea of it that I had formed in prospect.

I have received some interesting letters about it already—yours not the least so. Swinburne writes, too enthusiastically for me to quote with modesty.
Believe me, with sincerest thanks for your review,

> Ever yours,
> T.H.

P.S. One thing I did not answer. The 'grimy' features of the story go to show the contrast between the ideal life a man wished to lead, and the squalid real life he was fated to lead. The throwing of the pizzle, at the supreme moment of his young dream, is to sharply initiate the contrast. But I must have lamentably failed, as I feel I have, if this requires explanation and is not self-evident. The idea was meant to run all through the novel. It is, in fact, to be discovered in *every*body's life, though it lies less on the surface perhaps than it does in my poor puppet's.

> T.H.

Letter from Thomas Hardy to Edmund Gosse, 20 November 1895

> Max Gate,
> Dorchester,
> November 20th 1895

I am keen about the new magazine. How interesting that you should be writing this review for it! I wish the book were more worthy of such notice and place.

You are quite right; there is nothing perverted or depraved in Sue's nature. The abnormalism consists in disproportion, not in inversion, her sexual instinct being healthy as far as it goes, but unusually weak and fastidious. Her sensibilities remain painfully alert notwithstanding, as they do in nature with such women. One point illustrating this I could not dwell upon: that, though she has children, her intimacies with Jude have never been more than occasional, even when they were living together (I mention that they occupy separate rooms, except towards the end), and one of her reasons for fearing the marriage ceremony is that she fears it would be breaking faith with Jude to withhold herself at pleasure, or altogether, after it; though while uncontracted she feels at liberty to yield herself as seldom as she chooses. This has tended to keep his passion as hot at the end as at the beginning, and helps to break his heart. He has never really possessed her as freely as he desired.

Sue is a type of woman which has always had an attraction for me, but the difficulty of drawing the type has kept me from attempting it till now.

Of course the book is all contrasts—or was meant to be in its original conception. Alas, what a miserable accomplishment it is, when I compare it with what I meant to make it!—*e.g.* Sue and her heathen gods set against Jude's reading the Greek testament; Christminster academical, Christminster in the slums; Jude the saint, Jude the sinner; Sue the Pagan, Sue the saint; marriage, no marriage; &c., &c.

As to the 'coarse' scenes with Arabella, the battle in the schoolroom, etc., the newspaper critics might, I thought, have sneered at them for their Fieldingism rather than for their Zolaism. But your everyday critic knows nothing of Fielding. I am read in Zola very little, but have felt akin locally to Fielding, so many of his scenes having been laid down this way, and his home near.

Did I tell you I feared I should seem too High-Churchy at the end of the book where Sue recants? You can imagine my surprise at some of the reviews.

What a self-occupied letter!

> Ever sincerely,
> T.H.

The Bookman (London), January 1896

After you have read 'Jude the Obscure,' your thoughts run in two separate channels cut by Mr. Hardy's two nearly separate purposes. Your opinion of the book will largely depend on which you regard as the main one. These purposes are wound in with the history of Jude and the history of Sue. Their histories are intertwined, but they are not quite inevitable to each other; and so, to a greater extent than in most tragedies, you can regard the two chief actors separately.

A work of the intensest human interest, it is not evenly strong: it has been written too much under the stress of feeling for that. Any discontent which is not roused by merely superficial causes, which is not finnicking, and any offence which the book may contain for timid readers, must arise, I think, from the story of Sue. Personally I feel no offence, and I speak for at least some women. But I am not sure if her championship might not have been bettered. In herself, she is one of Mr. Hardy's stimulating women. He is particularly anxious not to shirk the consequences of her temperament, of that free spirit of hers that gave so willingly when not coerced by laws and authority. But in exhibiting the results of this temperament acting on her circumstances—her shilly-shally-ing, her contrariness about the marriage tie—there is an amount of exaggeration, or of reiteration, that becomes nearly absurd, as did the fickleness in the hero of 'The Pursuit of the Well-Beloved.' There is here something more than the 'series of seemings, or personal impressions,' spoken of in the preface. There is downright propaganda, which is always unconvincing, and even loosening to the convictions of the already converted. Sue is a woman that excites and leads. She is influential; her opinions and feelings do not need much emphasis and repetition. When they are given these, she becomes too much of a pamphlet and platform victim of the cruel marriage bond. Sue could love, and was not well fitted for marriage life. There she is not so very abnormal, and this would be the sooner admitted had Mr. Hardy not taken so much trouble to justify her running to and fro between Phillotson and Jude. But I admit this is a cold reception to a warm protest; and the fault of the novelist one may readily forgive to the man of feeling, sending his chivalry bravely out in new directions.

But the book is not made up of theories and examples of theories. The title is truly descriptive. Jude is the real subject; and Jude's story is among the most notable of Mr. Hardy's work. In his greater books—and this is one, undoubtedly —he has a way of passionately identifying himself with the aims or the sorrows of one personage, whom he loves in his blackest, his sinfullest, his pitifullest moments. That he does so, and that he does not hide such moments, make him one of the very grimmest and most sympathetic of all novelists. Tess, the Mayor, Clym Yeobright, and now Jude, are of the company. Jude's history is written as life writes a history, some features being traced from the beginning, while later, from hitherto unstirred depths, circumstance calls up the others. He is a man with the defects of his amiable virtues and his sensitive nature. There is only one woman in the world for his love and reverence, but if she be not there, his loneliness may seek less good company. In strong drink he has sometimes found a refuge from overtaxed nerves. Life finds out the weak places in his very human body and soul. He is, too, and especially, a man of the people with the native instincts of the scholar. The poetry of his aspirations, the disinterestedness of his pursuit, the undyingness of his passion, are made living to you, and some of the self-taught man's vanity and his laboriousness of expression are not suppressed. You think he must be cured for ever of his ambition that day when, having received the 'terribly sensible' repulse from the head of Bibliol College, he stood at the Crossway, and 'began to see that the town life was a book of humanity infinitely more palpitating, varied, and compendious than the gown life,' and at that supreme moment when he, the obscure craftsman, wrote along the wall of the dull college from whence the repulse had come, 'I have understanding as well as you.' But the passion is in his blood. He wanders round and round the sacred places like a moth round a candle. Christminster scenes mark the stages of his struggling, aspiring life. The imaginative child, watching from the roof of the Brown House the far-off spires and domes, the night-wandering stonemason 'under the walls and doorways, feeling with his fingers the contours of their mouldings,' the ghosts of old scholars, comrades of his solitude, are striking pictures out of his early, hopeful time. In his sick and unfortunate days, when forced to labour at an earlier-learnt trade than his own, he, as Arabella says, 'still harps on Christ-minster, even in his cakes,' shaping these with grotesque pathos to a reminiscence of traceried windows and cloisters. There, too, he dies, lonely and obscure, to the hum of a college chapel organ, and the shouts of Commemoration games. A poor workman to the end, a boyish imprudence for which he never shirked the payment, dogged him persistently; and the woman who had been his light and leader left him in the darkness, to fulfil, for superstition's sake, a loathed duty.

His career may wholesomely astonish some middle-class readers, inasmuch as it goes to prove that aspiring and sensitive souls do not need generations of literary education and genteel incomes to breed them; and that poverty and the stress of life reveal to such sensitive souls a world that the comfortably-placed and the unimaginative only deny because they have been saved and denied the chance of entrance.

Sue's story is a reality, with some unhappy exaggeration about it; but all that concerns Jude, in his strength and weakness, is masterly and written out of a deep heart. The constant lover—constant for all the Arabella incidents—makes, perhaps, widest appeal for sympathy. But it is another Jude on which Mr. Hardy has shed the full light of his imagination; and the wandering, rejected scholar flits a pathetic ghost through college gate-ways and by college walls for evermore. A. M.

The Bookman (New York), January 1896

'A Novel of Lubricity'

. . . The characters of the book are Jude Fawley, a peasant by birth, who is possessed of an intense yearning which is never gratified, for scholarly distinction, and of refined and spiritual traits which exist side by side with a lurking love of sensuality and drink; one Arabella, a typical barmaid, coarse, brazen, and cunning; Jude's cousin Sue, an Anglicised version of one of Marcel Prévost's *demi-vierges;* and a certain village schoolmaster named Phillotson, who has some unexplained sexual peculiarities at which Mr. Hardy, for a wonder, only hints. Jude is tricked into an early marriage with Arabella, and Sue is forced into one with Phillotson. Both marriages are ended by divorce, whereupon Jude and his cousin live together in unlawful relations, until an accumulation of disasters converts Jude into a sceptic and Sue into an hysterical *dévote*, whereupon they separate, Sue remarrying her schoolmaster as a matter of conscience, and Jude remarrying Arabella as a matter of desperation.

Such, in brief, is an outline of the story, which, even as Mr. Hardy tells it, is improbable, but which one would not criticise were it not for his extraordinary lack of reticence in the telling. There is nothing in the plot that justifies the grossness with which he has chosen to elaborate its details. Nor is this grossness the grossness of the English novelists of the last century—of Fielding and Smollett—with whom Mr. Hardy has many traits in common. It does not suggest the rude virility of young and lusty Englishmen, with huge calves and broad backs and vigorous health; of strapping fellows who roar out their broad jokes over a mug of ale in the tap-room of a country inn. It is rather the studied satyriasis of approaching senility, suggesting the morbidly curious imaginings of a masochist or some other form of sexual pervert. The eagerness with which every unclean situation is seized upon and carefully exploited recalls the spectacle of some foul animal that snatches greedily at great lumps of putrid offal which it mumbles with a hideous delight in the stenches that drive away all cleanlier creatures. We do not desire to dwell upon this subject. Our great objection to it is that it is wholly unnecessary, that in forcing us to batten upon such carrion, Mr. Hardy is sinning against light and wilfuly marring our appreciation of his grasp upon higher and nobler qualities than are the attributes of a scavenger.

. . . The fact is that Mr. Hardy tries to ride two horses—to be at one and the same time a romanticist and a realist, demanding for himself the romanticist's license in plot and the realist's license in incident. The result is a book that has none of the recognised claims to high literary rank; for it neither teaches a useful lesson, nor is it true to life. It is simply one of the most objectionable books that we have ever read in any language whatsoever.

. . . Some time ago we asked a distinguished critic what he thought of one of the younger of the French naturalistic novelists. 'Oh,' he said, carelessly, 'he is merely speculating in smut.' The expression is a crude one, and we should, perhaps, apologise for writing it down here; yet it serves our purpose excellently well, for in our judgment frankly and deliberately expressed, in *Jude the Obscure* Mr. Hardy is merely speculating in smut. *P.*

[?THE EDITOR, PROF. HARRY THURSTON PICK]

The Saturday Review, 8 February 1896

It is doubtful, considering not only the greatness of the work but also the greatness of the author's reputation, whether for many years any book has received quite so foolish a reception as has been accorded the last and most splendid of all the books that Mr. Hardy has given the world. By an unfortunate coincidence it appears just at the culmination of a new fashion in Cant, the Cant of 'Healthiness.' It is now the better part of a year ago since the collapse of the 'New Woman' fiction began. The success of 'The Woman Who Did' was perhaps the last of a series of successes attained, in spite of glaring artistic defects, and an utter want of humour or beauty, by works dealing intimately and unrestrainedly with sexual affairs. It marked a crisis. A respectable public had for a year or more read such books eagerly, and discussed hitherto unheard of topics with burning ears and an air of liberality. The reviewers had reviewed in the spirit of public servants. But such strange delights lead speedily to remorse and reaction. The pendulum bob of the public conscience swung back swiftly and forcibly. From reading books wholly and solely dependent upon sexuality for their interest, the respectable public has got now to rejecting books wholly and solely for the recognition of sexuality, however incidental that recognition may be. And the reviewers, mindful of the fact that the duty of a reviewer is to provide acceptable reading for his editor's public, have changed with the greatest dexterity from a chorus praising 'outspoken purity' to a band of public informers against indecorum. It is as if the spirit of McDougallism has fled the London County Council to take refuge in the circles called 'literary.' So active, so malignant have these sanitary inspectors of fiction become, that a period of terror, analogous to that of the New England Witch Mania, is upon us. No novelist, however respectable, can deem himself altogether safe to-day from a charge of morbidity and unhealthiness. They spare neither age nor sex; the beginner of yesterday and the maker of a dozen respectable novels suffer alike. They outdo one another in their alertness for anything they can by any possible measure of language contrive to call *decadent*. One scarcely dares leave a man and woman together within the same corners for fear of their scandal; one dares scarcely whisper of reality. And at the very climax of this silliness Mr. Hardy, with an admirable calm, has put forth a book in which a secondary, but very important, interest is a frank treatment of the destructive influence of a vein of sensuality upon an ambitious working-man. There probably never was a novel dealing with the closer relations of men and women that was quite so free from lasciviousness as this. But at one point a symbolical piece of offal is flung into Jude's face. Incontinently a number of popular reviewers, almost tumbling over one another in the haste to be first, have rushed into print under such headings as 'Jude the Obscene,' and denounced the book, with simply libellous violence, as a mass of filth from beginning to end.

If the reader has trusted the reviewers for his estimate of this great novel, he may even be surprised to learn that its main theme is not sexual at all; that the dominant motive of Jude's life is the fascination Christminster (Oxford) exercises upon his rustic imagination, and that the climax of its development is the pitiless irony of Jude's death-scene, within sound of the University he loved—which he loved, but which could offer no place in all its colleges for such a man as he. Only as a modifying cause does the man's sexuality come in, just as much as, and no more than, it comes into the life of any serious but healthy man. For the first time in English literature the almost intolerable difficulties that beset an ambitious man of the working class—the snares, the obstacles, the countless rejections and humiliations by which our society eludes the services of these volunteers—receive adequate treatment. And since the peculiar matrimonial difficulties of Jude's cousin Sue have been treated *ad nauseam* in the interests of purity in our contemporaries, we may perhaps give her but an incidental mention in this review, and devote ourselves to the neglected major theme of the novel. . . .

It is impossible by scrappy quotations to do justice to Mr. Hardy's tremendous indictment of the system which closes our three English teaching Universities to what is, and what has always been, the noblest material in the intellectual life of this country—the untaught. Sufficient has been quoted to show how entirely false is the impression that this book relies mainly upon its treatment of sex trouble—that it is to be regarded as a mere artistic and elaborate essay upon the great 'Woman Who' theme. That is really as much criticism as is needed here just now. The present reviewer will not even pretend to taste and dubitate, to advise and reprimand, in the case of a book that alone will make 1895 a memorable year in the history of literature. . . .

The Yorkshire Post, 8 June 1896

(A letter to the editor from Bishop William Walsham How)

Bishopgarth, Wakefield.

Sir,

Will you allow me to publicly thank you for your outspoken leader in your to-day's issue denouncing the intolerable grossness and hateful sneering at all that one most reveres in such writers as Thomas Hardy?

On the authority of one of those reviews which you justly condemn for this reticence, I bought a copy of one of Mr. Hardy's novels, but was so disgusted with its insolence and indecency that I threw it into the fire. It is a disgrace to our great public libraries to admit such garbage, clever though it may be, to their shelves.

I am, sir,
Yours, &c.,
WM. WALSHAM WAKEFIELD

Acknowledgements

Grateful acknowledgement is made to the following sources for material used in these units:

Text

Jennifer Gosse for Edmund Gosse, 'Hardy the Degenerate'; The Trustees of the Hardy Estate for the two letters from Thomas Hardy to Edmund Gosse dated 10th and 20th November, 1895; The Trustees of the Hardy Estate, Macmillan, London and Basingstoke, The Macmillan Company of Canada Ltd and The Macmillan Company, New York for Thomas Hardy, *Jude the Obscure* and for 'The Old Workman' in *Collected Poems*, © 1925 by the Macmillan Company.

Illustrations

Dorset County Museum; L. Harrison Matthews; Henry Mimms Collection, Bodleian Library Oxford; National Portrait Gallery; Oxford University Museum; Taunt Collection, Oxford City Libraries.

The Nineteenth-century Novel and its Legacy